Russia

Russia

BY STILLMAN D. ROGERS

Enchantment of the World
Second Series

SENN THOMAS
MIDDLE SCHOOL

Children's Press®
A Division of Scholastic Inc.

NEW YORK   TORONTO   LONDON   AUCKLAND   SYDNEY
MEXICO CITY   NEW DELHI   HONG KONG
DANBURY, CONNECTICUT

Frontispiece: Nenet girl, Siberia

Consultant: Dr. Amy J. Johnson, Ph.D., Assistant Professor of History, Berry College, Mount Berry, Georgia

Please note: All statistics are as up-to-date as possible at the time of publication.

Book production by Herman Adler Design

Library of Congress Cataloging-in-Publication Data

Rogers, Stillman, 1939–
    Russia / by Stillman D. Rogers.
      p. cm. — (Enchantment of the world. Second series)
    Includes bibliographical references and index.
    ISBN 0-516-22494-8
    1. Russia (Federation)—Juvenile literature. [1. Russia (Federation)] I. Title. II. Series.
DK510.23 .R64 2002-01-31
947—dc21   2001047724

Acknowledgments

The author would like to thank Dorothy Howard and other members of the reference staff at the Keene Public Library in Keene, New Hampshire, for their tireless persistence in tracking down accurate and up-to-date details about this rapidly changing nation.

Cover photo:
St. Basil's Cathedral,
Red Square, Moscow

Contents

Summer palace

Matryoshka dolls

Land of the Czars

Summer palace

T HE BRIGHT SWIRLING SPIRES OF ST. BASIL'S CATHEDRAL and the shining gold domes of the Kremlin tower over Red Square in Moscow. Against the same skyline are the grim, straight lines of massive gray buildings constructed during the Soviet era. Their austere shapes form a stark contrast to the flamboyant Czarist churches and palaces.

Czars and privileged nobles lived their lives on a golden stage all about these structures. Their capital at Moscow was filled with all the riches that money could buy. Peter the Great's new capital city at St. Petersburg was even more beautiful; there, canals spanned graceful bridges and were lined with pastel-colored palaces.

Opposite: **View of St. Basil's and Moscow**

Fountain at the Summer Palace, Petrodvorets

Peter the Great introduced Russia to more than just beautiful buildings. He also brought in musicians from the great cities of Europe to play at his court, he built royal theaters and concert halls, and he encouraged native composers to create music to be performed in them.

Golden fountains spouted in the gardens of Petrodvorets, a palace outside St. Petersburg. Inside the Winter Palace, grand staircases led the nobility, dressed in velvets, furs, and glittering jewels, to ballrooms where they danced to the finest music of their day. At Easter, they exchanged golden eggs studded with precious jewels.

The czars' world of music and parties and jeweled Easter eggs was not free, of course. Their lavish existence was bought by the sweat of peasants who owned no land and were little better than the slaves who worked for the rich nobles.

Nearly a century ago, in 1917, the Russians ended the rule of the colorful czars, whose luxurious lifestyle had robbed the people of a decent livelihood. The people now put their hope in communism, a system that promised to provide for them fairly, based on the common results of their labor.

Sadly, however, the Russian people only ended up trading one set of uncaring masters for another. Life for the common people was one of oppression under both sets of rulers. Years later, the Russian people could be proud that the Soviet Union put the first man into space and won rows of gold

Russian peasants prepare to harvest crops.

Geopolitical map of Russia

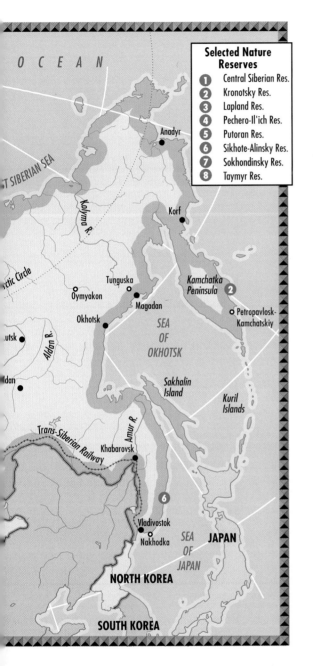

Selected Nature Reserves
1. Central Siberian Res.
2. Kronotsky Res.
3. Lapland Res.
4. Pechero-Il'ich Res.
5. Putoran Res.
6. Sikhote-Alinsky Res.
7. Sokhondinsky Res.
8. Taymyr Res.

medals at the Olympics, but they were still hungry, still overtaxed, and still unable to get decent housing.

After the end of over seventy years of communist rule, today's Russians, finally liberated from the excesses of both the czars and the Soviets, have taken the first steps toward freedom. Nonetheless, the long legacies of the czars and the Soviets—for better or worse—live on in this fascinating land.

Just as the czars fell to make way for the Soviets, the Soviet Union dissolved to make way for new freedoms for the Russian people. In the eyes of most Russians, these new freedoms shine even brighter than the gold domes of the Kremlin.

A Land in Two Continents

R USSIA IS THE LARGEST COUNTRY IN THE WORLD, COV- ering more than 6.63 million square miles (17 million square kilometers). It has the longest borders of any country in the world—22,539 miles (57,792 km). From the *oblast* (province) of Kaliningrad in the west to the Bering Strait in the east, it stretches 5,400 miles (9,000 km) across part of Europe and all of Asia.

On the north Russia faces the frozen expanse of the Barents Sea, Kara Sea, Laptev Sea, and the East Siberian Sea, all which are part of the Arctic Ocean. On the east, the Bering Sea separates Russia from the state of Alaska, only 49 miles (78 km) away. The North Pacific Ocean also borders on the east, as well as the Sea of Okhotsk and the Sea of Japan.

Ural Mountains

Russia's Neighbors

The long chain of the Ural Mountains separates the two conti- nents in which Russia lies. Their western slopes are in Europe, while on the east, Russia stretches all the way across the Asian continent.

Along the south, Russia borders North Korea, China, Mongolia, Kazakhstan, and the Caspian Sea. On the western side, from south to north,

A Land in Two Continents **15**

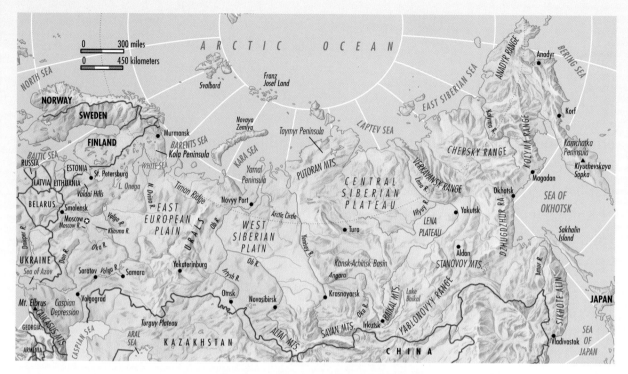

Russia's Geographical Features

Highest Elevation: Mount Elbrus, 18,510 feet (5,642 m), in the North Caucasus Mountains, also the tallest in Europe

Longest River: Lena, 2,734 miles (4,400 km)

Largest Lake: Lake Baikal, the largest freshwater lake in the world, 12,162 square miles (31,500 sq km) and 5,370 feet (1,637 m) deep, south of the Central Siberian Plateau between the Sayan and Yablonovy Mountains

Largest City: Moscow, population 9 million

Hottest City: Astrakhan, on the Caspian Sea, 88°F (31°C) July

Coldest City: Oymyakon, in Siberia, -96°F (-71°C) December

Length of Borders: 22,539 miles (57,792 km), the longest in the world

Length from East to West: 5,400 miles (9,000 km)

Highest Dam: Rogun Dam at Vakhsh Russia, 1,099 feet (335 m) high, volume, 98,750 cubic yards (75,500 cu m), also the highest and eighth largest in the world

Biggest Meteor: 1,543 pounds (700 kg) Krasnojarsk meteorite, fragment, Eniseisk, Siberia

Russia borders Azerbaijan, Georgia, the Black Sea, Ukraine, Belarus, Latvia, Estonia, the Baltic Sea, and Finland.

Most of the oblasts, regions, republics, and territories that make up Russia are in European Russia, west of the Ural Mountains. Each of these jurisdictions covers a small amount of territory, but those in the East European Plain tend to have larger populations. The republic of Mordovia, for example, has an area of only 10,218 square miles (26,200 sq km) but has a population of 964,000.

The oblasts east of the Urals are all much larger in area but have very small populations. Sakha, in north-central Siberia, is the largest republic in the federation, with a land area of 1,209,000 square miles (3,100,000 sq km). This is twice the size of Alaska, but its population is only 1,077,000.

European Russia: A Great Plain

Most of European Russia is part of the vast East European Plain that spreads from Ukraine, Poland, and Belarus eastward to the Urals. Aside from some low hills and mountains, the land is flat and open, suitable for the growing of crops.

Europe's tallest mountain, Mount Elbrus

Between the Black and Caspian Seas, the Caucasus Mountains mark the southern edge of European Russia. In this southern section, three great rivers flow from the north into the Black Sea: the Dniester, the Dnieper, and the Don. The Dniester and the Don begin their journey far north, forming a great means of water transportation. In the North Caucasus Mountains, Mount Elbrus stands 18,510 feet (5,642 m), the tallest in Europe.

**Trees on a sandy bank
on the Volga River**

The Volga River, 2,455 miles (3,960 km) long, begins to
flow in northern Russia's Valdai Hills, in the Kalinin region. It
flows east, then south, winding along the foothills of the Ural
Mountains and into the Caspian Sea. It has been a highway of
commerce since early times.

The northern part of the East European Plain borders the Barents Sea north of the Arctic Circle. This is a land of cold temperatures and ice with a slim border of tundra. It has bare rocky shores and flat, treeless land with a few low rolling hills. The soil is poor and will only grow low bushes, lichens, herbs, and mosses. Few people live here, except in Murmansk, a city on the Kola Peninsula. Murmansk is a major Russian port and naval facility. Even though it is inside the Arctic Circle, its port is ice free because of the warming influence of the Gulf Stream, a warm ocean current.

Ships docked at the commercial Murmansk seaport

Mountain ranges of the Kola Peninsula

The Kola Peninsula is very mountainous, with rich oil and gas deposits. These resources are also plentiful in much of the Volga-Ural area, south to the Kazakhstan border. European Russia has large deposits of iron, particularly near a feature known as the Kursk Magnetic Anomaly. The magnetic anomaly is a result of the large deposits of iron that cause compass needles to read incorrectly. The Urals provide Russia with copper, asbestos, tin, gold, and lead. There are also coal deposits, and the rivers provide hydroelectric power.

Looking at Russia's Cities

St. Petersburg, at the east end of the Baltic Sea, was built by Peter the Great in 1703 as a completely new capital for Russia. It now has a population of about 5 million people. The average daily temperature in summer is a mild 68° Farenheit (20° Celsius), and in winter it is 19°F (-7°C). Many Russians consider St. Petersburg the cultural capital of Russia. Its best known art treasures are found in the Hermitage. The huge dome of St. Isaac's Cathedral (above) can be seen from all over the city. On the other side of the Neva River, the Peter and Paul Fortress once guarded the city and was also a prison for opponents of the czars and, later, of the Soviet government. St. Petersburg, built on a river delta, is made up of many islands connected by ornate bridges. Visitors and local people enjoy riding on tour boats through the waterways to see the bridges and the palaces that overlook the water.

Novosibirsk began as a new city built in 1893 along the tracks of the Trans-Siberian Railway. It is the largest city in Siberia, with a population of 1.5 million. It lies on the southern side of the West Siberian plain, on the Ob River. Although it is in the south, the cold of Siberia keeps its summer temperatures at an average of 66°F (18°C) and a cold 6°F (-14°C) in the winter. Not a beautiful city, Novosibirsk has experienced tremendous growth in the past century and is known for its active academic and scientific community. The Novosibirsk Opera and Ballet Theater has one of Russia's best ballet schools, which local people support by attending the performances. The Alexander Nevsky Cathedral is the oldest stone building in the city. Visitors also like to see the Chapel of St. Nicholas, which can be found at the geographical center of Russia.

Asian Russia: Where East Meets West

Siberia is the huge mass of land east of the Ural Mountains. It's a place of great contrasts, huge plains, plateaus, and great mountain ranges. Like European Russia, it has startling temperature extremes.

Directly east of the Urals lies the West Siberian Plain, more than 780,000 square miles (2 million sq km) of flat land stretching east to the Yenisey River. Along the north, the Yamal Peninsula juts into the frigid Kara Sea, north of the Arctic Circle. The Turgay Plateau and the Altai and Sayan Mountains are on its southern borders.

Plains, plateaus, and mountains in Siberia

Three primary river systems run through this plain. The Irtysh River starts in Kazakhstan and flows north past the city of Omsk before joining the Ob River. The Ob rises in the Altai Mountains and then flows north past the city of Novosibirsk. From there it travels across the center of the West Siberian Plain and into the Kara Sea. The

Yenisey River

Yenisey starts in the Sayan Mountains, a bit further east, and flows north along the foot of the Central Siberian Plateau and into the Kara Sea. The Yenisey River is 3,435 miles (5,540 km) long, including the Selenga River headwaters.

Changing City Names

During the Soviet years, many city names were changed to those of Soviet heroes. When the Soviet Union dissolved in 1991, many cities' names again changed. St. Petersburg was named for Saint Peter when Peter the Great founded it in 1703. When World War I broke out, people thought that "burg" sounded too German, so they changed its name to the more Russian-sounding Petrograd, which means Peter's City. When Vladimir Lenin, the founder of the Soviet Union, died in 1924, Petrograd became Leningrad. However, when Russia became Russia again in 1991, the people wanted to return to the beginning, and so once again, it's St. Petersburg.

Another major city that changed its identity was Stalingrad, named for the Soviet dictator. In 1589 it was known as Czaritsyn, but it took Stalin's name in 1925. After Soviet Premier Nikita Khrushchev denounced Stalin for the murderous dictator that he was, the people adopted the name of their river and the city became Volgograd in 1961.

Oil burns at a West Siberian oil field.

Lake Baikal is the largest freshwater lake in the world.

The West Siberian Plain is a rich source of minerals and other resources. Some of the largest oil and natural gas reserves in the world lie under it. During the 1950s and 1960s Soviet leaders encouraged large-scale agriculture in the fertile part of the plain in the Virgin Lands Program. Although it opened large areas to wheat and other grain crops, it created serious ecological problems of erosion and pollution.

East of this area is the Central Siberian Plateau, bordered on the west by the Yenisey River Valley and the Putoran Mountains. On the south lie the Sayan Mountains, and east of Lake Baikal lie the Yablonovy and Stanovoy Mountains. Lake Baikal is the largest freshwater lake in the world, covering 12,162 square miles (31,500 sq km) and reaching 5,370 feet (1,637 m) in depth. On the east end of the plateau, the weather influence of the Bering Sea and the Pacific Ocean is blocked by the Verkovansk, Chersky, and Anadyr Mountains. The highest mountain in Asian Russia is Mount Klyuchevskaya Sopka, 15,525 feet (4,750 m) tall. It is an active volcano on the Kamchatka Peninsula.

A Big Bang

Early in the morning of June 30, 1908, as people in the Tunguska area of Eastern Siberia were beginning to go about their daily chores, a huge fireball and explosion suddenly filled the blue morning sky. Trees were knocked over like Popsicle sticks and fell in circular patterns. Fires broke out and smoke filled the air. People more than 300 miles (482 km) away felt the explosion and saw the smoke. About 35 miles (56 km) away, people were knocked over and houses were damaged, and 20 miles (34 km) away people were thrown through the air, one even landing in a tree. This was long before missiles and atomic bombs, so what could it have been?

Scientists are now pretty sure that it was a large piece of an asteroid entering the atmosphere from outer space. The asteroid piece was probably about 55 yards (50 m) in diameter and traveling about 7 to 12 miles (12 to 20 km) per second as it entered the atmosphere. The stress of its entry was so great that it exploded into tiny bits before it reached the earth. Although it left no crater, tiny dust-sized pieces of it were embedded in the trees.

The Central Siberian Plateau and the mountains surrounding it are sources of many minerals, including iron, antimony, mercury, gold, lead, and diamonds. The Tungus and Kansk-Achinsk Basins of the plateau and the Lena Plateau farther east also have large coal deposits. Oil and natural gas fields lie under the Lena Plateau and extend south to Irkutsk at Lake Baikal.

The plateau's rivers carry waters from the surrounding mountains north into the Laptev Sea. The largest is the Lena River, which rises in the Baikal Mountains before flowing 2,734 miles (4,400 km) northeast to the sea. The Vilyui starts on the north side of the Central Plateau and flows east until it meets the Lena. The Aldan River begins at the base of the Stanovo range of mountains, circling along the mountain bases until it joins the Lena.

Thick forests serve the timber industry.

Much of northeastern Siberia lies north of the Arctic Circle, with large areas of tundra extending from the northern shore into the mountains. South of that, vast woodlands stretch south into the middle West Siberian Plain and into the Central Siberian and Lena Plateaus. These forests are harvested for lumber to produce paper and other products.

Temperature and Its Effects

One of Russia's unique features is the wide variation in temperature from its north to its south. The seas in the north are all part of the Arctic Ocean system and are frozen much of the year. In the far south, temperatures are subtropical and there are even deserts. The mid-region is a temperate zone, where

The Ecological Legacy of the Soviet Union

The "ecological disaster" that the new government inherited from the Soviets was one of Boris Yeltsin's biggest concerns when he became president. Air, water, and ground in much of the country had been affected by pollution. Fish die in the chemical-filled rivers, and those that survive are unsafe to eat. Hundreds of big industrial developments pour pollutants into the Volga, which is further contaminated by runoff of agricultural chemicals.

Chemical and industrial waste flow into the Caspian and Black Seas, polluting them so that their fish are dying too. In the far north, entire areas that were once green forests are now miles and miles of gray tree stumps because the land has been poisoned by metal from two nickel factories (pictured). The courses of rivers were changed to irrigate the vast wheat farms, causing the inland Aral Sea to shrink dramatically, contaminating the surrounding lands with dust and salt.

Frozen seas create a
pressure ridge in Siberia.

temperatures are very low in winter and high in summer. Tall mountains in the south keep the Pacific and Indian Oceans from influencing the climate. In the north, there are no mountains to protect the country against the cold Arctic weather.

Across much of Russia, winter is the longest season. Over half of Russia is above the 60th parallel, and 45 percent of the land has permafrost. Snow covers St. Petersburg as many as 160 days a year, and rivers as far south as Moscow are frozen from late November to mid-April. In northern and eastern Siberia, rivers are frozen as long as 250 days of the year, leaving them mostly useless for transportation.

In the winter the winds blow from the south and southwest, across much of the country. In summer the winds blow from the north and northwest. This means that most places get cold weather in winter and moderate, cool temperatures in summer. Average winter temperatures are 16°F (-8°C) in St. Petersburg, -18°F (-27°C) in the West Siberian Plain, and -46°F (-53°C) in Verkhoyansk (in the eastern part of Siberia). In summer, St. Petersburg enjoys temperatures of 70°F (21°C), and Moscow is a few degrees warmer. At the same time, Irkutsk, in the southern part of the Central Siberian Plain, registers 70°F (20°C). In northeastern Siberia at Verkhoyansk, summer temperatures run about 63°F (17°C).

Permafrost

The northern parts of Russia are so cold that the ground has a layer that is always frozen. This is called permafrost because only the upper layer (called the active layer) thaws in the summer. Permafrost occurs inside the Arctic Circle as well as at very high elevations. It is hard for people living in these areas to farm or construct buildings.

Tundra, Taiga, Forest, and Steppe

E

ACH OF RUSSIA'S FOUR ECOSYSTEMS—TUNDRA, TAIGA, forest, and steppe—has its own animal and plant life, but as the seasons change wildlife moves along the fringes from one ecosystem to another.

Opposite: **Reindeer at their winter pastures**

Tundra

Northern Russia is in the tundra zone, where the soil is permanently frozen (permafrost). This zone starts as a narrow strip, including the Kola Peninsula and a strip along Karelia, dipping farther south in Siberia all the way to the Bering Strait.

A few feet of soil thaws in summer allowing shrubs, short-lived flowers, grasses, mosses, and lichens to grow. Tree roots cannot reach into the permafrost and have only a few weeks each year to grow. Walrus and seals are found in the waters of the cold and frozen northern seas and feed on the rich supply of offshore fish. On land (and on sea ice) polar bears roam, joined by arctic fox, reindeer, musk ox, and lemmings. Ptarmigan, snowy owl, and raven live on rodents such as the tiny lemming.

Walrus huddle in the cold and frozen waters.

Muskrats can be found in the taiga.

Taiga

In the band just below the tundra, the permafrost layer begins deeper in the ground, so that trees can sink their roots farther into the soil. Trees that grow in the taiga are firs, pines, and other evergreens, as well as larches. Forests cover much of the land, and swampy areas are common. Almost one-third of all the world's forests are in this region of Russia.

Elk, brown bear, sable, and fox roam these forests. Smaller species such as the marten, ermine, squirrel, and muskrat dodge their predators. During the summer weeks some of these animals go into the tundra looking for food.

ARCTIC OCEAN

NORWAY

FINLAND
Murmansk

St. Petersburg

Yukutsk

Moscow
Kazan

Samara
Yekaterinburg

Novasibirsk

Krasnoyarsk

KAZAKHSTAN

CHINA
Vladivostok
JAPAN

Four Ecosystems

Tundra   Taiga   Forest   Steppe

Meet the Russian Brown Bear

To many people, the brown bear symbolizes Russia. Big, strong, and able to fend off its enemies, the bear is covered in thick brown fur that makes it look almost playful and cuddly. The brown bear is far from cuddly though, and can be very dangerous. Bears like to live alone, are strong swimmers, and eat fish, small animals, wild honey, green plants, and berries. They can grow to be very large—an adult bear can weigh 300 to 600 pounds (140 to 275 kg) and can run at speeds up to 30 miles an hour (50 km/hr).

Bears in the wild can live up to thirty years. In the past, Eurasian bears were caught and trained to perform in circuses and shows, and some were even taught to dance to music.

The taiga zone is about 370 miles (600 km) wide and runs across the Russian European and Asian continents, widening out in Siberia. Along the southern side of the band, birch trees grow. In the taiga are reindeer, wolves, brown bear, elk, beaver, lynx, fox, sable, and the maral deer. Because this region is low and swampy, it also buzzes with mosquitoes, gnats, and midges, which feed the native bird life.

Siberian lynx

Forest

The taiga slowly melds into the forest zone, the next band to the south. This part of the environment has been exposed to industry and development, and pollution has killed much of its wildlife. Forests here are much like those seen in the United States and other temperate zones. Birch, maple, and oak mix

Perseverance and Preservation

Russia has 160 government-controlled nature reserves dedicated to preserving the ecology of the country. The largest is Putoran Reserve in the Krasnoyarsk Territory, along the western edge of the Central Siberian Plateau. It has an area of 7,283 square miles (1,887,000 hectares) and contains 38 species of animals, 142 bird species, and 650 plant species. Also in the Krasnoyarsk Territory is the Taymyr Reserve with an area of 5,207 square miles (1,349,00 ha) and the Central Siberian Reserve, which is 3,752 square miles (972,000 ha).

One of the oldest reserves, founded in 1930, is the 2,787 square mile (722,000 ha) Pechero-Il'ich Reserve in the Komi Republic in western Russia. It has 46 species of animals, 215 species of birds, and 702 species of plants. Many of the animals and birds in the reserve are endangered, and conservation programs help to preserve them. For example, in 1927 there were no European bison left in the wild and only forty-seven lived in captivity. However, a breeding program has built up their numbers to more than 3,000. Today, wild European bison herds now live in the Caucasus Mountains.

with conifers and larger shrubs to provide food and homes for small game. Brown bear were once common in this zone, but hunting and loss of forest have made them rare. You can still find roe (a kind of small antelope), wolves, fox, and beaver.

An egret perches in the
tall grass.

Steppe

The steppe is a region of mostly flat plains that stretch across
European Russia and lie in a band east of the Urals to the
plateau region. Its rich black soil makes it good for farming.
Temperatures here are moderate, and the growing season is
longer than other parts of Russia. Animals found here are
small, such as mice, hamsters, mole-rats, and squirrels. Birds
are common and in the Volga Basin are cormorants, geese,
and egrets. Once wild horses and deer roamed the Siberian
steppe, but they are now extinct.

At the foot of the mountains that form Russia's southern borders are dry and desert areas. In the deserts roam a unique type of gazelle, and small rodents hide from the sharp eyes of predator birds.

Russia's Mega Lake

Lake Baikal (sometimes spelled Baykal), in the south-central part of Siberia, is an amazing place. Not only is it the largest freshwater lake in the world—12,162 square miles (31,500 sq km)—but it is the oldest, estimated to be 25 million years old. One-fifth of all the fresh water in the world is in this lake, which is fed by more than 300 rivers and streams. It has 1,200 species of plants and animals that are found nowhere else. One of the unique animals is the nerpa (pictured), the only freshwater seal in the world. The lake is also famous for sturgeon, a fish that produces the eggs prized as caviar. Heavy pollution by industry along the shore, however, threaten the life of the lake and its wildlife.

In the mountains are more forests and a richer wildlife. South of the plains and desert in European Russia are the Caucasus Mountains, a high range with more than 6,000 varieties of plants. Tur (mountain goat), bezoar (wild goat), mouflon (mountain sheep), red and roe deer, chamois (a kind of deer), and wild bison that were brought back from extinction live on the mountainsides. In the Sayan, Altai, Baikal, and Stanov Mountain

Red deer are indigenous to the mountains.

ranges, in the south of Asian Russia, are the Manchurian and Caspian tigers, leopards, raccoon dog, Manchurian hare (rabbit), elk, musk deer, sable, and brown bear.

Deer and Perfume

Siberia is the home of the musk deer, which is quite different from deer found in North America. The males do not have horns or antlers, instead they have long protruding teeth like walrus tusks. The males also have a gland that produces musk, a substance important in making perfumes.

The females also are a bit different. When a baby musk deer suckles its mother, it raises its forefoot and touches the rear leg of the mother, something other deer do not do. Musk deer are a threatened species because their habitat is being destroyed and because of hunting.

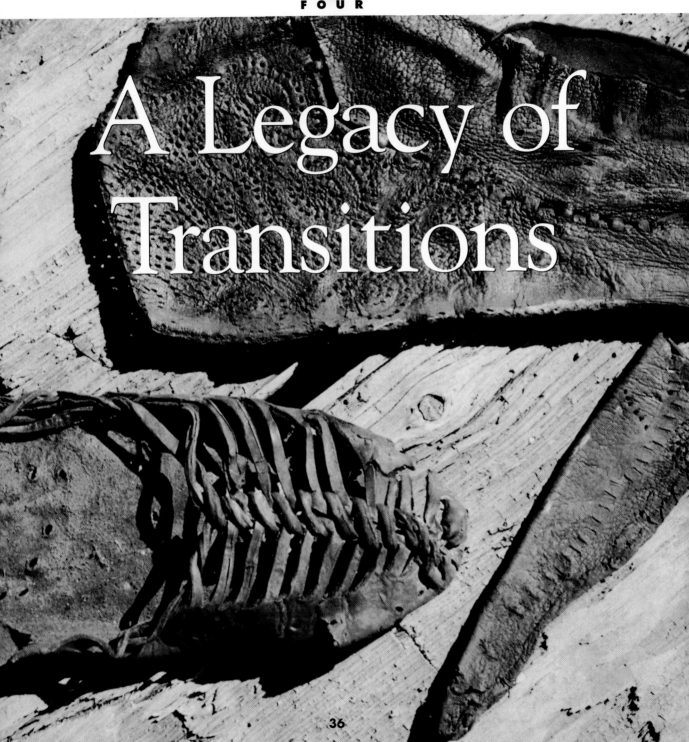

A Legacy of Transitions

Archaeologists have discovered that by A.D. 600 Slavic farmers, herders, beekeepers, and trappers called Rus lived around Kiev in Ukraine. The Rus expanded north and west and later were joined by Scandinavian people called Varangians, who used the rivers to trade with countries in the Mediterranean region.

Opposite: **Archaeologists uncovered this child's leather shoe in Novgorod.**

A Leader for the Rus

Around A.D. 860 the Rus, who had no government, asked the Varangians to help them establish a state to protect them from attack. They chose Rurik, a Varangian, as their leader. His

The Rus invite Rurik to be their leader.

descendants ruled for the next 800 years. Their capital was Novgorod, near the Baltic, and later Kiev in the European plain.

The Rise and Fall of Kiev

Early leaders placed trusted men, usually princes and relatives of the leader, in charge of towns and cities outside Kiev. When these early leaders died, lower ranking ruling nobles from different parts of the country fought one another for control, especially of Kiev. These landholding nobles, whose wealth and power had depended on the ruler of Kiev, gained more independence and control, forming almost separate countries without a central loyalty. These internal wars destroyed trade and wealth, and the people suffered from famine.

By the early 1200s, Russia was a small principality, and power had passed from Kiev to the Grand Duke of Suzdal. He was weak and could not control the strong princes in nearby cities and towns who were almost independent of him.

Batu Khan

The Golden Horde Takes Over

In 1223 the first wave of Tartars, known as the Golden Horde, invaded from Mongolia. They withdrew but swept back over most of Russia twelve years later led by Batu Khan, grandson of Ghengis Khan.

Batu Khan imposed the methods of government that the Mongols had developed in Asia. Under the Tartars, all Russians had to register with the government to be sure they paid taxes. Foreign agents were appointed to collect the new taxes. The Khan decided who the Russian leaders would be, charged heavy taxes, and made local Russian rulers pay tribute. The Khans' methods were brutal.

Tartar control of Russia left a deep mark on government and the people. It was from the Tartars that the idea of a strong autocratic central government took hold and remained even into the twentieth century. Their system of bureaucracy financed by tribute and heavy taxes became accepted as normal.

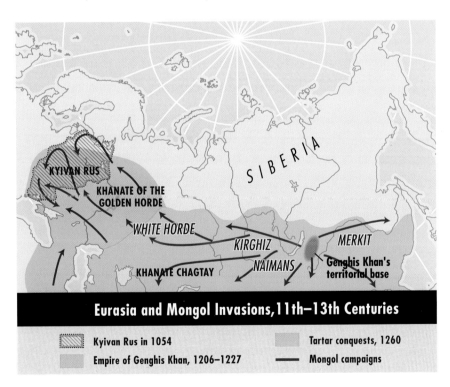

Eurasia and Mongol Invasions, 11th–13th Centuries

Kyivan Rus in 1054

Empire of Genghis Khan, 1206–1227

Tartar conquests, 1260

—— Mongol campaigns

Rendering of Moscow, mid-fourteenth century

Ivan III

The Rise of Moscow

A small town in the 1100s, Moscow became a principality in its own right in the late thirteenth century. The second Grand Prince of Moscow, Ivan I, worked closely with the Tartars, collected taxes for them, and increased his power over other regional leaders. The power of Muscovy (Moscow region) grew stronger when a later Grand Prince, Dimitri, defeated the Tartars in the battle of the Don.

The First Czar

Tartar power was dwindling by 1480. Around this time Ivan III (The Great), Grand Prince of Muscovy, gained control over many nobles and he began the process of bringing the former Kievian territories together again. He was the first ruler to call himself Czar (Russian for Caesar) and Ruler of All Rus.

Before Ivan III, the nobility owned land outright. Ivan III ended that system, granting lands to nobles only for military and administrative service to the czar. Under his new laws, nobles did not own land and could not pass it on upon their death unless their heirs renewed their vows of service. Another change involved the peasants use of land: now the new landlord was entitled to part of their crops. Peasants could also be sent to the army to fill the landlord's obligation to provide soldiers to the military.

Power became more centralized under the later czars, as more of Kievan Rus was reclaimed. Czar Ivan IV (The Terrible, 1533–1584) solidified the authority of the czar and established autocracy (the total rule of one person or group). He appointed a Zemsky Sabor—council of administrative officials, landlords, church officials, and even some peasants— to weaken the nobles. Its members had no authority and could only advise the czar.

A meeting of the Zemsky Sabor

It was during Ivan IV's reign that the single greatest expansion of Russian territory began. Between 1558 and 1697 Russia took control of the vast lands to its east, extending Russia across the Asian continent and even into Alaska.

Rurik's Dynasty Ends

After Ivan IV died, Russia suffered "The Time of Troubles," when many people competed to become czar. Russia was torn by invasions of two separate impostors claiming to be Dimitri, a "lost" son of Ivan IV. It was at this point that the dynasty of Rurik came to an end.

The laws of Ivan IV were rewritten by later czars, further strengthening the autocracy. Oppression and intolerance reigned as foreign artisans and craftsmen who had once flourished in Russia were now restricted, the church's independence was threatened, and the state claimed the right to control private property. The peasants were not even mentioned.

To end the unrest, a new Zemsky Sabor met in 1613 and selected a sixteen-year-old nobleman, Michael Romanov, as czar. The Romanov dynasty would last until the monarchy ended in 1917.

Peter the Great

In 1682, Peter I became co-czar at age 10 with his brother Michael. Since they were both children, however, their older sister ruled for them. Michael died in 1689 and at age 17 Peter reigned alone. His rule brought great changes to Russia and finally opened it to the West.

Peter had learned of European ideas from foreign merchants outside of Moscow. Fascinated by military and Western technology, he gathered many Europeans about him as advisors. His first priorities were to reorganize Russia's army on the European model, to build a navy, and to strengthen the country's access to the sea. Peter even worked as a laborer in Dutch shipyards so he could bring back knowledge of how to build ships.

Looking to the Baltic Sea as the best place to gain a port, and to become a great power, Peter captured Swedish territories and founded St. Petersburg in 1703 as Russia's new capital and all-weather port. In 1709 Peter again attacked the Swedish army at the battle of Poltava, soundly defeating them and ending their threat to his new Baltic territories.

Western experts were brought in to improve mining, manufacturing, and farming. The life of the peasant grew worse as new

Peter I lays out plans for St. Petersburg.

laws allowed factory owners to buy peasants as workers and heavy new taxes were imposed on the people but not on nobles and clergy. Westernization did not please all of Russian society, however, with many people resisting the changes.

Expansion of the Russian Empire, 1462–1914

Russia, 1505	Acquisitions by 1725	Acquisitions by 1914
Russian Empire, 1598	Acquisitions by 1796	19th-20th century sphere of influence
Acquisitions by 1689	Acquisitions by 1855	

Nonetheless, Peter dragged Russia, kicking and screaming, into the modern age.

Catherine the Great

When Empress Catherine II (The Great) took the throne in 1762 she continued westernizing and expanding Russia as Peter I had. By the end of her reign in 1796, the nobility was heavily influenced by European literature, music, ballet, architecture, engineering, and the military. Catherine divided

Russia into provinces based on population, giving each an administration, courts, and police. After an unsuccessful peasant rebellion she extended serfdom.

The Troublesome Nineteenth Century

Russia faced a desperate threat in 1812 when Emperor Napoleon of France invaded Russia. Napoleon captured Moscow, but the long freezing Russian winter and the people's resistance weakened the French army so badly that only 30,000 of Napoleon's 600,000 men made it out of Russia alive.

By the time Alexander II became czar (1855), the need for economic reforms in Russia had become critical. Therefore, in 1861 he freed 22.5 million serfs from private ownership, giving them fifty years to pay for their freedom and land. Two

The French army battling the harsh Russian winter.

years later, he freed government-owned serfs and gave them land. He also created provincial and local councils in which all classes were represented. Censorship and state control of education were reduced, and jury trials were introduced.

When Alexander II was assassinated in 1881, his heir, Alexander III, responded by limiting the people's rights. He promptly reversed many of his father's reforms and tightened censorship. A secret police (*Okhrana*) was established and liberal Western ideas were now scorned.

As a result of this repression, people became increasingly critical of the czar and his government. Educated Russians— including social democrats (called KD or Kadets), socialists, and the more extreme anarchists, who believed in no government—began to call for political reform. In 1898 radical socialists organized outside of Russia.

When Nicholas II followed his father as czar in 1894, educated people tried to convince him to allow a constitution. Nicholas refused and continued his father's repressive policies.

The Twentieth Century

In 1904 Russia occupied Manchuria, and Japan attacked Russia's army. Russia's disastrous defeat in that war, together with the heavy taxes and poor economic conditions resulting from the war, caused even more hardship for the already downtrodden people. Sensing the dangerous political climate that had developed, many leaders called for democratic reform.

In January 1905, a large and peaceful crowd marched to the Winter Palace in St. Petersburg to present a petition to the czar in which they asked for better living conditions and lower taxes for the poor. In response, the palace guards, on horseback, fired into the crowd killing hundreds. This "Bloody Sunday" massacre made the people even angrier, and they formed committees (soviets) to work for reform.

Worried by this serious turn of events in 1906, the czar agreed to form an elective assembly, the Duma. The czar's power was absolute, however, and when the new Duma favored reforms that he didn't approve of, he simply dismissed it. He then dismissed the second Duma until finally the third Duma (1907) and the fourth Duma (1912) were under his control.

Palace guards attack petitioning crowds during the "Bloody Sunday" massacre.

A Senseless World War

In 1914 an Austrian war on Serbia triggered a series of alliances leading to the eruption of World War I and to Germany's declaration of war on Russia. With Russia's entry into the war, its internal problems only worsened. The army was completely unprepared for war militarily. Food and supplies were in short supply both on the battlefront and at home,

Czar Nicholas II at the battlefront

Russian mystic Rasputin

and taxes were increased even more. The czar, ignoring domestic problems and unrest, went to the battlefront to direct Russian forces. Few people saw any reason why Russia should be involved in the war at all. When news of heavy loss of soldiers' lives was combined with the enactment of heavy taxes, the people's opposition to the war increased.

Revolution Strikes Russia

The fate of Russia's royal family was sealed when Czarina Alexandra fell under the influence of Grigory Novykh, a peasant mystic, nicknamed Rasputin because of his lustful reputation. Rasputin appeared to ease the czar's son's hemophilia (a dangerous blood condition) and gained extraordinary power over the czar through the czarina. Both the people and nobles considered Rasputin evil and a bad influence on the czar and lost their trust in the czar. In February 1917, when the people rioted in the capital, the royal guard turned their rifles on their officers rather than fire on the people. With the loss of their loyalty, the czar was forced to give up his throne.

The Mystery of Anastasia

After Czar Nicholas lost his throne in 1917, he and his family were taken to Ekaterinburg in Siberia where they were all shot to death in July 1918. Before long, rumors began to spread that one of their four daughters, Princess Anastasia, had managed to escape. For many years a woman named Anna Anderson claimed to be Anastasia. She met with several relatives of the Romanov family but most of them never accepted her as the real Anastasia. She died in 1984. Several books and two movies, the latest being a Disney film, kept the mystery alive for almost a century, although DNA tests have now confirmed that she was not Anastasia. In 1991, the remains of nine bodies were exhumed, tests proved that they included the remains of the czar, his wife, and three of their daughters. Two bodies were not found—the Czarevich Alexei and one of his sisters.

The fourth Duma formed a new government headed by Alexander Kerensky, a Social Democrat. Soldiers and workers, who had never had any say in the government before, formed councils called soviets that influenced the decisions of the new government.

The new government could not decide what it should do about the war with Germany. While radical revolutionaries wanted to end the war, the new government sought to defeat Germany. Since reform programs were slow to take effect, the most radical soviets cried for immediate action, urging the peasants to seize land and factories.

A Second Revolution

In April 1917, the German High Command allowed Vladimir Lenin, leader of the majority Socialists (Bolsheviks), to go through Germany in a sealed rail car from western Europe to St. Petersburg, hoping he would end the war with Germany. In May, Leon Trotsky, exiled leader of the minority Socialists (Mensheviks), arrived from the United States. Together with

Vladimir Ilich Lenin (1870–1924)

Vladimir Lenin, the son of a middle-class teacher, was a Marxist revolutionary influenced by his older brother Nikolai, who was hanged for his part in a plot to assassinate Czar Alexander III.

In 1895 Vladimir was exiled to Siberia for revolutionary activity. When released, he spent years working on his theory of Marxism, writing *What Is to Be Done*, his vision of the role of Socialists in the creation of Marxist states. He was again forced into exile in Europe until 1917.

Returning to Russia after the February 1917 revolt, he plotted against the new government and led the Bolsheviks in overthrowing it in November. He then became leader and began the total restructuring of the Russian state. He died in 1924 and his body was preserved in a glass coffin in his tomb in Moscow's Red Square. For decades, visitors streamed by his coffin daily as a show of loyalty to the communist ideal.

Joseph Stalin, they began to undermine the Kerensky government. The military supported them, and on November 7, 1917 (October 25 on the Russian calendar then in use), the three men seized power and established a communist government.

In 1918 the new Soviet government took over all lands from the nobles, the church, and even the peasants. No one was allowed to own land. Banks were seized, and workers took over factories. Food supplies were controlled, with the state selling and distributing nearly all basic goods.

New regional and provincial Soviets were established to administer the government and special courts, and a new secret police, the Cheka, was formed to deal with resisters and sabotage. The army was reorganized, and a separate peace was signed with Germany. Peasants farmed the land as state workers, and in 1919 the first state-owned collective farms, where workers had no ownership rights, were opened.

Russia Gets a Constitution

In 1918, a new constitution was written first for Russia; later, additions covering the other areas and people controlled by Russia were also included. Under the new government, the Federation of Soviet National Republics, authority was placed in the All-Russian Congress of Soviets, which chose the high officials. Only laborers, soldiers, and peasants could vote, and all parties except the Communist Party were outlawed. Several other nationality republics joined Russia in 1922, forming the Union of Soviet Socialist Republics (USSR).

Workers of the World, Unite!

Lenin's Bolsheviks tried to spread their ideas by supporting worker revolutions in foreign countries. When they began to hold international meetings (*Cominterns*) to overthrow governments around the world, other countries came to fear Russia and isolated it from trade and international affairs.

Meanwhile, in 1921, shortages of food, clothes, and housing forced the government to back off from some reforms. Farmers were again allowed to sell their produce, and some small factories became privately owned. The economy began to improve.

Leon Trotsky (second from left) and Joseph Stalin (far right)

A Struggle for Power

After Lenin's death in 1924, his followers struggled for control. Trotsky, a more radical Communist, competed with Stalin, who was more practical. As head of the Communist Party, Stalin won and had Trotsky exiled and eventually murdered.

The Five-Year Plans

In 1928 Stalin began the first Five-Year Plan to improve production. The state took over all planning and established specific production goals. All farms were made into collectives (*kolkhoz*) where committees decided how to reach the state's goals. No one was allowed to make personal profit from their own labor.

The Five-Year Plan tried to eliminate all private enterprise by ending credit, raising rents, stopping shipments, imposing taxes, and discriminating against business owners and their families. Unofficially, Stalin began a program to destroy wealthier peasant landowners and shop owners (*kulaks*) by intimidation, imprisonment, exile, and murder. Millions were killed.

Peasants thresh wheat on a collective.

Attacks on the Russian Orthodox Church and other religions were encouraged during the first Five-Year Plan. A League of Militant Atheists spread antireligious propaganda, people were harassed and pressured not to attend church, priests were attacked, and churches were turned into warehouses.

The Economy Improves

The plan succeeded and was followed by new Five-Year Plans until World War II delayed economic development. Until the war, conditions improved gradually. Food became available, but it cost more. Housing was hard to find and small apartments housed several families, not just one.

The Second World War

Until 1939 the Soviet Union had been politically cut off from Europe. Even after the European powers allowed Hitler to destroy Czechoslovakia in 1938, they were slow to ask Russia to join them when Hitler threatened Poland. To protect itself and to provide a buffer of land against Germany, the Soviet Union and Nazi Germany agreed to destroy Poland and divide it between them. After invading Poland in 1939, the Soviet Union seized Finland's eastern provinces.

On June 22, 1941, the German army attacked the Soviet Union, and Soviet troops retreated slowly, destroying everything that the Germans could use as they went. Like Napoleon's troops the century before, the German army was slowed by the fierce cold of Russian winters. Near Leningrad, Moscow, Sevastopol, and Stalingrad they were stopped.

Russia Joins the Western Allies

After being attacked, the Soviet Union was quick to join European nations and the United States against Germany. Foreign aid, mostly from the United States, brought military equipment and supplies. By 1944, the German army was in retreat. The war ended for the Soviet army when Berlin, the German capital, fell in May 1945. More than 20 million Soviets were killed in the war, and the countryside was devastated.

An Iron Curtain Falls

After the war, Germany was divided into zones. The United States, Great Britain, and France controlled western Germany, and the Soviet Union occupied Poland, Latvia, Lithuania, Estonia, Czechoslovakia, Romania, Hungary, and Bulgaria. Western Germany had a freely elected government, but in their zone the Soviets immediately installed dictators friendly to them. The Soviet-controlled national police crushed all democratic opposition. All of Eastern Europe and half of Germany fell under control of the Soviet Union.

A Cold War With the West

In 1946, England's prime minister, Winston Churchill, said, "An iron curtain has descended across the continent." Europe had been divided into two parts, one free and the other controlled by the Soviets. The "iron curtain" separating the West and the communist states lasted from 1946 until 1991, a period known as the cold war.

Tensions between the Soviet Union and the West increased steadily after World War II. Fearing the Soviets' territorial ambitions, the nations of Western Europe joined the United States to prevent Soviet expansion in Europe and around the world. The Soviets were aggressive, trying to create a revolution in Greece and then to force the Allies out of their zones of occupation in Berlin, Germany. The borders between the two sides were soon closed and an arms race began. People feared that a real war could begin at any time.

Under Stalin the Soviet Union made great industrial advances and stabilized the Soviet government. But the social fabric of Russia was destroyed by Stalin's iron rule. Progress came at the expense of the people's freedoms and living standards. The iron-bound rule of the communist elite created a corrupt privileged class that was as blind to the people's needs as the old nobility had been. When Stalin finally died in 1953, the people hoped for better times.

After Stalin

The leaders of the Soviet Union after Stalin's death were Georgi Malenkov (1953–1955), Nikita Khrushchev (1955–1964), Leonid Brezhnev (1964–1982), Yuri Andropov (1982–1984), and Mikhail Gorbachev (1985–1991). All but Gorbachev followed policies that continued the cold war. All attempts by the East Europeans to loosen Soviet control were crushed by the Soviet army.

In 1979 the Soviet Union invaded Afghanistan. That war lasted until 1988, resulting in a cost so huge in terms of money

Andrei D. Sakharov (1921–1989)

Andrei Sakharov was a world-class physicist and a philosopher. He created both the hydrogen bomb and the reform movement in Russia. In 1950 he became part of the secret Soviet atomic bomb team, and by 1955 he had designed and tested the first Soviet hydrogen bomb. Proclaimed a "Hero of the Soviet Union," he became one of the elite with special privileges.

Sakharov, however, worried about the dangers of radiation and of nuclear war. He therefore urged the Soviet leaders to stop nuclear testing, and he spoke out in favor of antimissile treaties and urged an end to the arms race. He used his position to help others in need. In 1970 he helped found the Moscow Human Rights Committee, which kept track of human rights abuses in Russia. In 1973 he earned the Nobel Peace Prize.

For leading the opposition to war in Afghanistan, Sahharov was exiled to the city of Gorky. After his release, he was a leader in the movement for a democratic government and was elected to the Congress of Peoples' Deputies. He died in 1989 while working on a new constitution.

and lives that average Russians began to oppose the war. As early as 1981, it was clear that major changes had to be made to save the Soviet economy.

Perestroika, Glasnost, and Gorbachev

Mikhail Gorbachev came to power in 1985 seeking *perestroika* (rebuilding) and *glasnost* (openness). He wanted to save the Soviet Union and the Communist Party by reforming the way

Mikhail Gorbachev aimed to rebuild and "open" Russia (Boris Yeltsin in rear).

both did business. He asked people to speak openly about problems and solutions, at last opening the gates of criticism and allowing people to voice their discontent. For the first time, too, the Soviet Union agreed to treaties reducing the number of nuclear weapons and missile systems. The cold war began to thaw.

Gorbachev's perestroika loosened government control over the economy, but as the government lost control over the economy, prices rose and goods became expensive and unavailable. Glasnost allowed Russians to learn the darker side of Soviet history: the repressions, concentration camps, and murders of the Stalin years in particular. In addition, the minorities within the Soviet Union began to challenge governmental authority. Perestroika and glasnost together brought into the open problems that had been growing beneath the surface.

Although Gorbachev intended perestroika and glasnost to strengthen the Soviet Union and the Communist Party, they had the opposite effect. They caused the destruction of both.

The Soviet Union Ends

Since the November revolution in 1917, Russia had been one of the many republics of the Soviet Union. Although Gorbachev was head of the Soviet government, the Russian

Republic had its own legislature, the Congress of Peoples' Deputies. One of its members was Boris Yeltsin. He favored greater Russian independence within the Soviet Union. On June 11, 1990, Russia declared itself a sovereign state within the Soviet Union.

When many member republics demanded independence, Gorbachev tried to reorganize the Soviet Union. In August 1991, conservative Communist Party leaders seized Gorbachev to prevent him from doing so. Yeltsin rallied the people against the coup's leaders, in support of Gorbachev, and after three days the coup failed. But now Gorbachev found that Yeltsin was in control of the government bureaucracy of the Soviet Union. Without control of the bureaucracy Gorbachev was almost powerless.

Russians cheer after the coup's collapse.

Boris Yeltsin and the New Russia

Yeltsin outlawed the Soviet and Russian Communist Parties in Russia and met with leaders of Belarus and Ukraine to form the Commonwealth of Independent States. A few days later, five central Asian republics, Armenia, and Azerbaijan signed the treaty. On Christmas Day 1991 President Gorbachev

The Commonwealth of Independent States

resigned, and the Soviet Union ceased to exist. Russia became an independent country.

When elected president of the Russian Federation in 1991, Boris Yeltsin became the first freely elected leader in Russian history. His election was a call for reform, so he wrote a new constitution containing many principles of constitutions in Western countries. The people approved the constitution by referendum vote in December 1993 and elected a new State Duma.

When former communist members of the legislature opposed his economic reforms, Yeltsin issued executive decrees, and in 1993 he dismissed the Duma. Many legislators refused to leave, leading to a military confrontation. After tanks fired on the legislative building (called the White House), however, Yeltsin prevailed.

In 1994 rebels in Chechnya (a republic of the Russian Federation) began terrorist attacks against Russian troops and

Sergei A. Kovalev (1930–)

people, and the Russian army was sent to stop them. In spite of several cease-fire agreements, that civil war still continues.

A Peaceful Change of Government

In December 1999 Yeltsin unexpectedly resigned as president, appointing Prime Minister Vladimir V. Putin to fill the remaining part of his term.

Putin, former head of the State Security Services, was a popular choice. A presidential election was held in 2000 in which Putin promised to fight corruption, reduce poverty, improve the economy, and support the military. He was elected and began his term by calling for a stronger central federation government, a respect for law, less governmental interference in business, protection of property rights, tax reform, and human rights, including freedom of the press.

Since becoming president, he has worked with the legislature to create a new tax system, and he has promoted legislation allowing the private ownership of land for the first time since 1917. President Putin remains popular with the Russian people.

After the September 11, 2001, terrorist attacks on the United States, President Putin joined with the United States and other nations around the world in a coalition to end terrorism. He has even allowed American armed forces to use former Soviet military bases.

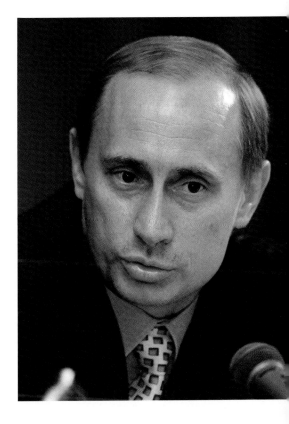

Russian's current president, Vladimir Putin

The Legacy of the Czars and the Soviets

FROM THE TIME OF IVAN IV, THE CZARS WERE ABSOLUTE monarchs who ruled by decree; their decrees and even their wishes were the law. This set the standard for a very strong central government.

Beginning in 1917, the communist governments took on similar powers. There were really two governments: the Communist Party and the Soviet Union, with the Communist Party the stronger of the two. Communist Party officials told the Supreme Soviet (legislature) what to do, and they obeyed. The government controlled every aspect of life, from social issues to industry. This led to inefficiency, waste, and corruption.

Opposite: **Statue of Lenin in front of the VDNKh, Moscow**

Meet Ivan the Terrible (1530–1584)

Ivan IV was only 3 when he became Grand Prince of Moscow in 1533. A regent ruled for him, but when he was 16 he had himself crowned czar. The following year he took control of the government. At first he gave people more voice in the government, but that was just to lessen the power of the nobles. Later his rule became harsh. Many people believe that the death of his wife, thought to have been murdered by his enemies, changed him into a cruel madman. He made the peasants into serfs, and his police attacked nobles, merchants, and even peasants, taking away property and executing those who got in his way. These violent attacks and murders earned him the nickname "The Terrible."

A Change in the Power Structure

Congress of Peoples' Deputies in session

From 1989 to 1993 the Soviet Union and Russia took the first critical steps in changing government from a tightly controlled dictatorship toward a democratic republic, a process that still continues today.

Russia's road from a dictatorial, centralized state has been long and difficult. Boris Yeltsin and Vladimir Putin have both struggled with a legislative body that feared change and wanted to retain the old ways of governing.

The struggle to build relationships between the central Russian Federation and the republics and regions continues. Debates about who should do what between the president, the State Duma, and the Federation Council also continue. The government has not yet figured out how business and property should be managed. But the system seems to be working. Even in bitter legislative and presidential battles the constitution has been followed, and there have been no coups since 1993. Reforms have continued to be made.

An Old Flag Returns

Russia's white, blue, and red banner was originally a flag for Russian merchant ships. It was created in 1697 by Peter the Great and was used until the Bolsheviks took over the government in 1917. Then the gold hammer and sickle on a red background was adopted. The historic tricolor flag was readopted after it was flown from the Kremlin walls on December 25, 1991, to mark the end of the Soviet Union.

The President's Job

Russia's government is divided into executive, legislative, and judicial branches. The president (executive) establishes domestic and foreign policy and, as the head of government, represents the country at home and abroad. The president can issue decrees that have the power of law without legislative review, he can dismiss the Duma (legislative branch), he can propose new laws to the Duma, and he can schedule referendum votes without legislative approval. The president also selects members of the judicial branch, the Constitutional Court, the Supreme Court, and the Superior Court of Arbitration, with approval by the Federation Council.

The Prime Minister

The daily operation of government agencies is controlled by the prime minister, who is appointed by the president with the consent of the Duma. The prime minister recommends the names of department and agency ministers to the president.

Moscow: Did You Know This?

Founded in 1147, Moscow was the capital until Peter the Great founded St. Petersburg in 1703. Again made capital in 1918, Moscow has been the capital of Russia, the Soviet Union, and the new Russian Federation.

Moscow's population of 9 million people makes it the largest city in Russia. In the summer its average temperature is a comfortable 70°F (21°C), but in winter it's a chilly 15°F (-9°C). Even in winter the streets are filled with people strolling by the river, in parks, and visiting the many sights of their city. Visitors go first to Moscow's centerpiece, the huge open stone-paved Red Square. Red Square is famous around the world as the place where a huge parade was held every May 1 to honor workers and display Soviet military power.

The walls of the ancient Kremlin fortress rise on one side with the tombs of Lenin and other Soviet leaders at its foot. At the end of Red Square the onion-shaped domes of Saint Basil's Cathedral swirl red, green, and orange like balloons in the sky. Inside the Kremlin walls churches and palaces of the czars sparkle with many large golden domes. Some government offices are also inside the Kremlin. Across the square is the GUM Department Store, an elegant arcade with a glass roof and some of the best shopping in Russia.

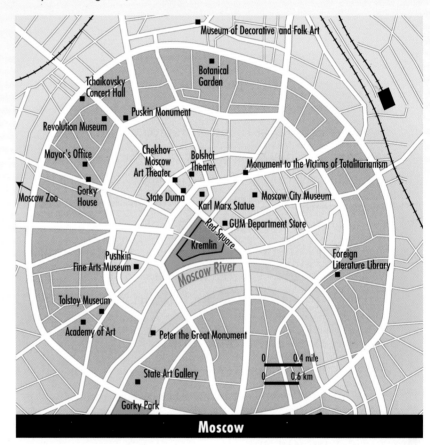

He and the ministers enforce the constitution, acts of the legislature, and presidential decrees that form the law of the country. They also prepare the government's budget, which the legislature must approve.

Russia's Legislative Branch

The legislature has a lower chamber, the State Duma, and an upper chamber, the Federation Council, consisting of two representatives from each province, region, or territory.

How Legislative Members Are Chosen

State Duma members are elected from districts throughout the country. The State Duma is a full-time legislative assembly. Its members are not allowed to hold other federal jobs or to be members of the assemblies of the member republics.

The governor (or president) of each region, oblast, or territory selects one member of the Federation Council who must be approved by the regional legislature. The other Federation Council member is elected solely by the legislature. By definition, members of the Federation Council are part-time and also hold office in their own subnational areas.

How the Duma and Federation Council Work

Each chamber elects a chairman and divides the work among committees, each of which is responsible for a certain subject. The State Duma must approve all bills for spending to operate the government, but the budget must first be approved by the president. The Duma and Council enact bills into law.

NATIONAL GOVERNMENT OF RUSSIA

Executive Branch

- PRESIDENT
- PRIME MINISTER
- CABINET

Legislative Branch

- DUMA (LOWER HOUSE, 450 MEMBERS)
- FEDERATION COUNCIL (UPPER HOUSE, 178 MEMBERS)

Judicial Branch

- SUPREME COURT (23 MEMBERS)
- COURT OF ARBITRATION (5 MEMBERS)
- CONSTITUTIONAL COURT (19 MEMBERS)

The Federation Council is in charge of the relationships between the provinces and jurisdictions. It also approves nominations to the three national courts and the appointment of the procurator general (the chief law enforcement officer, similar to the United States' attorney general). The Council approves treaties, reviews the Duma's tax and budget bills, and considers issues of war and peace.

Russian Justice

The Supreme Court, the highest court in Russia, hears civil, criminal, and administrative cases, some of which originate there but most of which are appeals from lower courts. The Superior Court of Arbitration hears mostly commercial and economic disputes and has divisions in cities and provinces. The Constitutional Court decides whether the laws, decrees, and orders of the legislative and executive branches are constitutional.

Court reforms have emphasized the independence of the courts, but some judges appointed under the former Soviet system still think in terms of policies of the old system. They are out of tune with efforts to bring fairness and equality to the legal system. Reform has included introducing jury trial in some cases, but this is not widespread yet.

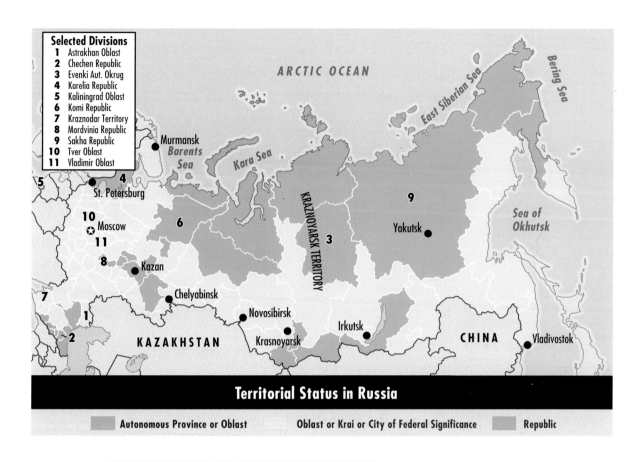

Selected Divisions
1 Astrakhan Oblast
2 Chechen Republic
3 Evenki Aut. Okrug
4 Karelia Republic
5 Kaliningrad Oblast
6 Komi Republic
7 Kraznodar Territory
8 Mordvinia Republic
9 Sakha Republic
10 Tver Oblast
11 Vladimir Oblast

ARCTIC OCEAN

Barents Sea
Kara Sea
East Siberian Sea
Bering Sea

Murmansk
St. Petersburg
Moscow
Kazan
Chelyabinsk
Novosibirsk
Krasnoyarsk
Irkutsk
Yakutsk
Vladivostok

KRAZNOYARSK TERRITORY

Sea of Okhutsk

KAZAKHSTAN

CHINA

Territorial Status in Russia

Autonomous Province or Oblast   Oblast or Krai or City of Federal Significance   Republic

The Provinces and Territories

Russia is a democratic federation of twenty-one autonomous (self-governing) republics, forty-nine provinces (oblasts), six territories, ten regions, one autonomous oblast, and two cities (St. Petersburg and Moscow), each of which has the status of an oblast. It was established by a constitution approved by the voters in a free vote in 1993.

Each of the republics, provinces, and territories has its own legislative body, usually called an Assembly or Duma, with members chosen by the people. The executive heads of the republics are usually called president or prime minister and are elected by the people. The executive heads of the oblasts, territories, and autonomous regions are called governors and are appointed by the president of the Russian Federation.

The Rights of Russians

Under the constitution of the Soviet Union, citizens had a very broad range of rights but these rights existed only on paper. In reality, those rights were few. The law was bent to suit the purposes of the Communist Party and the state. State influence over the courts was heavy. Many citizens were sentenced to prison or to exile with little regard for their rights.

Voting was a new civil right given to the people.

Constitutional Rights

The new constitution of 1993, adopted by the vote of the people, restates those rights and adds many more. Russians were quick to use their new rights to express themselves and claim the civil rights that are now theirs.

The constitution declares all citizens to be equal regardless of race, creed, sex, nationality, or political belief. The right to the ownership of private property was included for the first time. This includes the right to inherit or pass on property. If the state needs to take private property, it must pay its reasonable value. Citizens have the right to religious freedom and the right of freedom of conscience. The rights of the several nationalities that comprise the republic are also recognized, and these include the right to use their own national languages in schools, newspapers, and broadcasting.

People can now travel and live anywhere and do not need government approval to move. They can meet peaceably, petition the government, and join in a protest. Freedom of the press, both written and electronic, is guaranteed. The tendency for government to want to control the news still exists, however. The prosecution of the owner of the largest independent TV network in 2000 led to questions about the government's commitment to freedom of the press.

Russian teens sell publications on the streets of Moscow.

The Economics of Oppression

RUSSIA'S ECONOMY HAS BEEN UNSTABLE FOR CENTURIES. Historically, the czars controlled both the land and those who used it. The people who farmed land did not own it but worked for the government or for a nobleman or a community organization (called a mir), which was responsible to the nobleman.

Even after industrialization in the 1800s, labor was still controlled by the czar and noblemen. Workers were paid little and received only meager supplies for themselves and their families. Although the serfs received some land when they were freed in 1861, the land was later taken away.

Opposite: **People stand in line for goods at the state-run GUM department store.**

Under the Soviet Union

The revolution in 1917 brought severe economic change. All private property was taken by the government, which planned and managed all business, agriculture, and industry. Central planning committees in Moscow determined how much of everything would be made and who would make it.

The Metric System

Russia uses metric weights and measures, as does Europe and much of the world (the United States does not). Distances and lengths are measured in meters or kilometers (1,000 m) and weights in grams or kilograms (1,000 g). A meter is divided into 100 centimeters. Other equivalents are:

1 meter	3.2808 feet
1 yard	.914 meters
1 kilometer	.6214 miles
1 mile	1.6093 kilometers
1 kilogram	2.2046 pounds
1 pound	.436 kilograms

Goods were not priced according to the cost to make them but by decree of a planning agency. At one time, bread was priced so far below the cost of its ingredients that farmers fed bread to their animals because it was cheaper than grain. Planning agencies paid little attention to what people actually needed.

Reform at Last

Mikhail Gorbachev's perestroika was meant to reform the system, but those reforms did little to improve a rapidly declining economy. They were, however, an important start to serious change. Boris Yeltsin rose to power because he recognized that even more basic changes were needed. He wanted to abandon the old Soviet economic structure and replace it with a free-market economy. He saw that Russia needed new laws creating property rights and regulating private business practices.

Russians stand in line at an ATM.

Changing Banks

State-controlled banking could not cope with a free-market economy. Credit was available only to state businesses, and there was no private credit system, such as credit cards or car loans. All private business dealt in cash because there were no checking accounts. An entirely new banking system had to be created.

The new Russian Central Bank was formed to control credit and money

What Is Inflation?

Inflation describes the loss of the value of a country's money. This loss is measured as a percentage of the value of the money. For example, if a loaf of bread cost 1 ruble at the beginning of the year and cost 1.20 rubles at the end of the year the inflation rate would be 20 percent. For Russia in 1993, the inflation rate was 2,000 percent. That loaf of bread that cost 1 ruble in January cost 2,000 rubles by December.

Inflation usually develops when the government prints and circulates large amounts of paper money. With more paper money and few goods to buy, prices rise. Early in the 1990s, Russia did not have enough money from taxes to pay its bills. Workers and people on pensions were not being paid. When the government began to print large amounts of money to pay them, the value of the ruble fell far and fast.

supply. Commercial banks were also created, former state banks were privatized, and many new banks were established.

Transforming the Russian economy was an enormous challenge. Planning had to shift from a central bureau to many individual decision makers. Price controls that held prices below the cost of making goods were removed, and the price of foods and goods shot up suddenly.

People bought less, yet state industry continued to stockpile goods that people could not afford to buy. Inflation became such a problem that it reached a level of more than 2,000 percent in 1993. At that point the Central Bank began to print more money and extended more credit to failing industries.

The Challenge to Industry

The Soviet's Five-Year Plans had concentrated on heavy industry and mining to meet military needs, especially during the cold war, and had ignored the needs of ordinary people. People needed clothes, furniture, and appliances, but industry wasn't providing them. The old Soviet-era factories and systems

Money Facts

The Russian unit of currency is the ruble (pronounced rOO-bl), made up of 100 kopeks. Because of runaway inflation after price controls were lifted, the ruble has been "redenominated," or decreased in value, several times.

People fear that this will happen again, so the ruble has very little value outside of Russia. People prefer "hard" currency, such as American dollars or German marks, because these will not lose their value overnight. In April 2002, US$1 was worth 31.20 rubles.

Coins for 1, 5, 10, and 50 kopecks show Moscow's iron horseman statue, whereas 1, 2, and 5 ruble coins have the Russian symbol of a double-headed eagle. Russia has paper notes in 5, 10, 50, 100, 500, and 1,000 ruble denominations. The center of the 5-ruble note pictures the Novgorod monument erected for the 1,000th anniversary of Russia, and the

10-ruble note shows a bridge over the Yenisey River in Krasnoyarsk. The 50-ruble note has a detail from a monument in St. Petersburg with the Peter and Paul Fortress in the background.

were inefficient and old-fashioned. State-owned business and industry needed to be privatized (taken over by nongovernment owners) in order to succeed.

The effect of this turmoil on Russia's economy was dramatic: between 1990 and 1995 the value of everything produced (gross domestic product) dropped 50 percent. Much of the loss was in defense-related heavy industries; the new Russian state simply could not afford its heavy cost. Many inefficient industrial plants closed once they lost the state support that kept them running.

The slowdown also meant lower demand for materials such as iron and steel. Although Russia led the world in steel production in the 1980s, in the 1990s production declined by about half. The Russian automobile industry suffers from the same problems. Demand is down, and old Soviet-style assembly and financial systems make Russian cars more expensive

Engine assembly line at an auto factory

than imported cars. In the mid-1990s it took the best Russian car factory thirty times longer to build a car than it took a Japanese factory. The auto industry was also hurt by the sudden drop in demand for military vehicles when the cold war ended. As early as 1993, one-third of the production of sixty-two major groups of consumer products, such as washing machines, turbines, and tractors, had dropped by half.

Textile manufacturing, the main industry of about fifteen cities, also suffered. By 1996 almost 70 percent of textile workers were out of work. Inflation had made the Russian worker's income so low that people could not afford to buy new clothing. All light manufacturing fell 48 percent by the mid-1990s, including the items people needed most, such as shoes and household items. Sales of these items also suffered due to the high inflation.

The Privatization Process

Privatization—changing a publicly owned company to a privately owned one—was done in several different ways. Sometimes workers were given the chance to buy small businesses. Other businesses were sold at public auction. The government also issued stock vouchers to 144 million Russians. Each voucher had a value of about US$63. Vouchers could be used to buy stock in companies being privatized, or they could be sold or invested. By 1994, 70 percent of large and medium-sized businesses and 90 percent of small businesses—employers of two-thirds of the industrial labor force—were privatized.

A privatized machine and tool factory

On the Farm

State and collective farms were also privatized, with very mixed results. On Soviet-era collectivized farms, farmers were state workers with no incentive to work harder or to improve farming techniques. The poor transportation system could not deliver farm produce to markets.

By 1996, a third of collective farms became businesses, organized much as they had been before reform. Most of the others became cooperatives or were turned into companies in which the workers owned stock in the company. Although privately owned farms are now allowed, the number has not grown as fast as experts expected. Only 5 percent of usable agricultural land was privately owned by 1995. Most of the reorganized farm businesses have still not started using more efficient practices, and transportation remains a problem.

Father and son on a small privatized farm

Russia's Assets

Russia is the largest country in the world, but its climate and geography limit what can grow there. Much of the land lies above the Arctic Circle. The Ural Mountains form a wall

Rural women raise chickens on their farm.

between European and Asian Russia, and the cold, rugged mountains of northern and southeastern Siberia are not good farmland. Only 10 percent of Russian land is suited to agriculture, and only 6 percent, or 1,642.22 million acres (667.7 million ha), are used for crops. The rest of the land is used for raising animals or remains unused. Approximately 15 percent of the population of Russia works in agriculture.

Grain harvest

The primary crops grown in Russia—grains such as wheat and barley—are raised in the north Caucasus, in the Don and Volga River basins, and in southwestern Siberia. Droughts, inefficient agricultural methods, supply shortages, and transportation problems all led to lower production during the 1990s.

What Russia Grows, Makes, and Mines

Agriculture (1998)

Potatoes	31,300,000 metric tons
Wheat	26,900,000 metric tons
Sugar beets	10,800,000 metric tons

Manufacturing (1990)

Nonelectrical machinery	US$130,956,000,000
Food products	US$85,868,000,000
Textiles	US$37,435,000,000

Mining (1997)

Coal	244,000,000 metric tons
Iron ore	70,800,000 metric tons
Palladium	47,000,000 metric tons

Russia's Forest Bounty

Forests are another great Russian asset, covering 1,887 million acres (764 million ha). Almost 22 percent of all the world's forests and almost half of the world's coniferous (cone-bearing trees, such as pine) forests are in Russia. More than three-quarters of these forests are in Asian Russia. With the economic problems of the 1980s and 1990s, more pressure has been put on forestland.

Tree-felling tractors remove trees.

Resources

▨ Cereals (wheat, barley, corn)	**B** Bauxite	**L** Lead	
▨ Cereals (wheat, rye, oats)	**C** Coal	**O** Oil/Gas	
▨ Dairy, Truck farming	**Cu** Copper	**Na** Salt	
▨ Pasture	**D** Diamonds	**S** Silver	
▨ Forests	**G** Gold	**T** Tin	
	I Iron	**Z** Zinc	

Easier access from the east and a need for hard currencies have led Russia to sell major timbering rights to Chinese, North and South Korean, and Mongolian companies. Ecological damage to Russian forests has been tremendous, but a $60 million project sponsored by the World Bank is aimed at protecting them by improving forest management and harvesting techniques.

Sputnik and Beyond

A postage stamp commemorating sputnik

Central planning made it possible to concentrate on perfecting the very successful Soviet space program, beginning with sputnik in the late 1950s and continuing to the space station of later years. Russia was the first nation to put a man, and later a woman, into space. Although that program has been cut back to concentrate on immediate needs, Russia has joined the United States and other nations in joint space ventures, including playing an important role in building the new international space station.

Transportation: Roads and Rails

In Western Europe and in the United States, highways and roads help transport goods and people from place to place. Russia has placed little emphasis on roads. By 1995 Russia had only 303,180 miles (489,000 km) of roads open for public travel, compared to more than 6.3 million miles (about 10 million km) of roads in the United States.

An Iron Road to Asia

The Trans-Siberian Railroad, begun in 1891, is one of the many wonders of Russia. It is 5,787 miles long (9,259 km) and runs from Moscow in the west to Vladivostok in the east. A journey from end to end takes about eight days. In its early years, the trains ran on tracks laid over the frozen waters of Lake Baikal in the winter and crossed the lake by ferry in the summer. The lake was bypassed in 1916. The Trans-Siberian Railroad opened up Siberia for settlement and exploration. It is used to transport timber, raw materials, and Siberian produce, and it also brings in most of the imports from Asia.

The most popular method to transport goods in Russia is by railroad. There are about 95,500 miles (154,000 km) of tracks covering the nation. Soviet planners put factories in politically important population centers rather than where the raw materials were mined. Railroads are an important factor in Russia's economy. Without them, materials could not reach factories and products of manufacturing and agriculture would not be able to be delivered to the cities.

A barge sails by the Kremlin on the Moskva River.

Waterways

Russia's 62,600 miles (101,000 km) of waterways are also an important part of the transportation system. Since the very beginning, the combination of rivers and canals has linked Russia together. Because of canals that connect rivers and lakes, you can board a ship in Moscow and travel to the

Baltic Sea by water. You can also travel down the Volga to the Caspian Sea or down the Don River to the Black Sea. The ships that transport goods also carry passengers.

The waterway system is limited, however, by the Russian climate, since ice closes it for many months every year. Russia has major ports at Murmansk, an ice-free port in the Arctic Ocean; at St. Petersburg and Kaliningrad on the Baltic; and at Vladivostok, Nakhodka, Magadan, and Petropavlosk-Kamchatskiy in Asia.

Energy to Spare

One of Russia's greatest assets is its supply of energy sources, but it uses energy so inefficiently that the country consumes much more than most countries in relation to the value of goods they produce. Some of the largest oil reserves in the world are in the Urals and in western Siberia. Russia is also a major producer of natural gas; it has been estimated that Russia contains 35 percent of all the world's natural gas.

A pipeline carries gas from wells to the refinery

Russia's coal reserves are thought to be 200 billion tons, which are also some of the largest in the world. Since mining coal requires a lot of labor, however, coal is more expensive than other energy sources. Declining demand from consumers and industry has hurt energy companies and all parts of the economy. The period of reform has been very painful for Russian coal workers who went on strike in the mid-1990s because they were unpaid for many months.

In Russia, inflation is being decreased and goods have become more affordable.

A Hopeful Outlook

Slowly, the government has been able to cut the country's inflation rate. By mid-2000 the take-home income of the average Russian had risen 8.7 percent over 1999 and more people had jobs. Whereas 9.73 million people had been unemployed in January 1999, the number had fallen to 9.12 million in February 2000. The figure is still high but is dropping steadily.

The value of goods made by the country's industries for the same period increased by 10.7 percent. Another positive sign was the 9 percent rise in the value of all goods and services produced in Russia during 2000. The economy slowed in 2001, with an increase of only 5 percent. At the same time inflation fell to 18.6 percent in 2001.

There is reason for optimism about the future of the Russian economy and the people's prospects for a better life. The economy seems to be headed upward as wages are rising and inflation is falling. Private foreign investment, though not as large as Russia had hoped, is growing as Russia adopts the laws, banking practices, and legal protections that businesses need to succeed. The World Bank, the United States, and the European Community have also invested heavily in Russia to help preserve its new democracy.

The Russian People

T HE RUSSIAN FEDERATION IS A COLORFUL BLEND OF MANY different nationalities and ethnic groups. These range from the tall blond people of Scandinavian background to those whose faces show their Asian or Persian ancestry.

About 82 percent are Russians, descended from early Slavic peoples. The rest are divided between more than 100 other ethnic groups. About 4 percent are called Tartars, descendants of the Mongols who invaded in the 1200s, and 3 percent are Ukrainians, from the nearby state that was once part of the Soviet Union. The Chuvash, descendants of Tartar people who lived near the Volga before the Mongol invasions, make up about 1 percent. While most of the minority groups speak their own languages, they also speak Russian.

During the Soviet era, particularly in Stalin's day, those who were not Russian were the target of the worst abuses by the communist government. Nearly every family can tell of some terrible thing that happened to relatives, ranging from being denied jobs, to exile, and even murder. Today the shadow of discrimination against ethnic minorities still lingers. Many people still speak badly of Jews and Chukchi (native people from the far corner of Siberia) and

Opposite: **Elderly couple from Siberia**

Who Lives in Russia?

Russians	82%
Tartars	4%
Ukrainians	3%
Chuvash	1%
Others	10%

The Russian people derive from many ethnic groups.

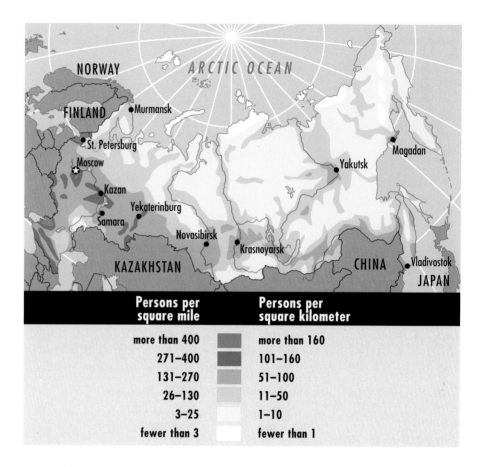

Persons per square mile		Persons per square kilometer
more than 400		more than 160
271–400		101–160
131–270		51–100
26–130		11–50
3–25		1–10
fewer than 3		fewer than 1

they are the subject of many unkind jokes. In bad economic times these minorities always suffer the most.

About 117 million of Russia's 150 million people live in the European part of Russia, and about three-fourths of these people live in cities. Nine million people live in Moscow, and 5 million in St. Petersburg. These and other cities have seen great surges of people moving from the country in search of jobs. Housing, health care, and food supplies have been strained even further by these new arrivals.

The Russian Language

Russian is a Slavic language but has its own letters, called the Cyrillic (pronounced ser-IL-ik) alphabet. About the time that Rurik became leader of the Rus, two missionaries from the Roman Catholic Church at Constantinople set out to convert the Slavs to Christianity. Between 855 and 885, Saint Cyril worked among the Slavs in the Crimea and Saint Methodius worked in Moravia. In order to translate the Gospels into the languages used by the Slavs, they created a new alphabet based on Greek letters.

Cyrillic is very different from the Roman alphabet used for English. Some of the letters resemble those in Greek, while some look (but do not sound) like letters in the Roman alphabet. Only A, E, M, C, and T look and sound much the same as English.

Cyrillic letters on advertising billboards

Common Russian Words and Phrases

Zdravstvuite (ZDRAST-voo-yet-eh)	Hello
Pozhalvista (pa-ZAHL-oos-ta)	Please
Da Svidanie (das-vee-DAHN-ya)	Goodbye
Da (dah)	Yes
Nyet (nee-et)	No
Spasibo (Spah-SEE-bo)	Thank you
Menia zovut ... (min-Ya-AH-za-VOOT ...)	My name is ...

The common alphabet and common religious heritage became important factors in bringing the Slavs together. Since the time of Cyril, the alphabet has been adopted throughout Russia and remains in use today.

Health and Health Care

Under the Soviets, health care was free for everyone, at least in theory. In reality, so little money was spent on the system that proper health care was available only to those who were able to pay for bribes or hire doctors privately. Public clinics did not even have basic supplies, and many had no running water. Children were not immunized for contagious diseases,

Russia's health-care system is in need of improvement.

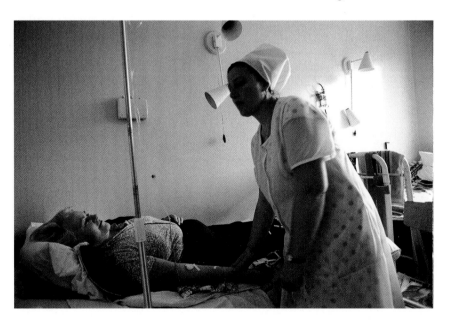

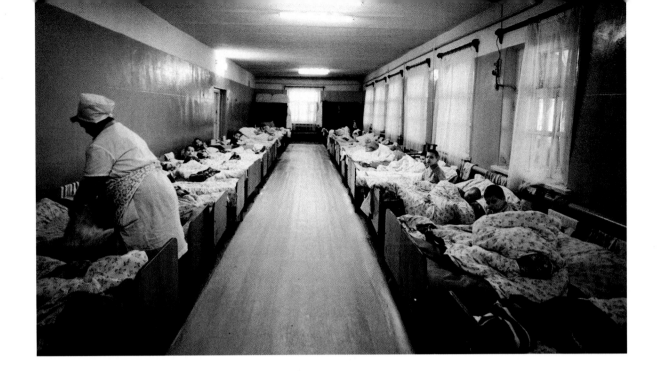

Orphans prepare for bed in
a state-run orphanage.

so epidemics spread easily. Despite recent efforts to improve it,
Russia's health-care system is still poor.

Russians are six times more likely to die of alcoholism or
related accidents than Americans. Alcohol is the third most
common cause of death in Russia. Work production hits low
points on Monday mornings, after workers have spent a weekend of drinking. Orphanages are overcrowded with children
removed from the homes of alcoholic parents.

Perhaps the most alarming health hazard of all is the effect
of seventy years of a government that stressed industrial
growth without considering the poisoning of its land, air, and
water. Eighty million Russians live in areas where air pollution
is above the danger level, and 30 to 40 percent of children
have diseases caused by polluted air. In the Kola Peninsula, on
the White Sea, one-fourth of all babies are born with serious
physical defects, and factory workers there have very high

Orphans prepare for bed in
a state-run orphanage.

rates of heart and lung disease and lead poisoning. One-third of the population of Magnitogorsk, the site of the world's largest steel mill, has lung diseases.

Moscow's infant death rate is twice that of the United States, a statistic that is blamed on the smokestacks of nearly 3,000 factories that pollute the city's air. Illness from nuclear contamination is almost impossible to estimate, a result of

Sunbathing amid polluting smokestacks

Some Health Facts

- In 1992 Russian scientists found that 15 percent of the land was unsafe for people because of toxic waste or nuclear accidents.

- In 1995 the education ministry stated that only 20 percent of Russian children were healthy.

- By age 40 the average Russian person has eaten more than 40 pounds (28 kg) of toxic chemicals in his or her food.

nuclear waste from ships scuttled in the northern seas, and accidents and explosions at plants, such as the Chernobyl nuclear power plant. This plant in the Ukraine exploded in 1986, spreading deadly nuclear contamination that reached the homes of about 2.6 million Russians.

The average life expectancy for women in Russia is seventy years, but for men it has fallen to fifty-seven years. Infant deaths are increasing, and almost half of Russian births have medical complications. The incidence of major diseases that threaten lives—tuberculosis, whooping cough, diphtheria, and others—has increased, and the nation's death rate is greater than its birth rate. The difference is so great that the population of Russia is expected to fall to 140 million (from 150 million) by 2005.

Education

Under the Soviets all Russian children had access to free education and were required to finish ten years of school. The result was a population with a very high literacy rate—99 percent in 1997.

The system is still much the same, with about half of all students continuing on to grades 10 and 11 after examinations. Higher scoring students follow one type of study, such as science, mathematics, or languages, while those with lower scores can learn a trade. About one-fourth of students continue on to university. Unfortunately, 87 percent of the better educated Russians emigrate or go abroad to work and live.

The dramatic changes in Russia with the fall of the Soviet government have affected education, too. Under the Soviets, all textbooks were controlled by the government, so they repeated the "party line" instead of giving a true account of history. When the news was allowed to report what was actually happening—and what had happened under communist rule—the information was so different from what was in the

Only one-quarter of students attend university.

textbooks that students didn't know what to believe. One year schools even had to cancel history examinations because the students did not know which version to use in their answers. Today, teachers explain these subjects, and, as schools are able to afford new books, the old ones are being replaced.

Students participate in a class discussion.

The most striking change is in the way children are now taught. Instead of memorizing what the teacher says, students in many schools are now encouraged to think and to ask questions. Russians see these new teaching methods as a way to make sure that their country will continue working toward a free society.

Translating Russian Names

Everyone has a first name, although children are called by a nickname. Ivan, for example, would be called Vanya by his friends and family, while Elena would be called Lena. Their second name is made up of their father's first name, with "ovna" added at the end for women and "ovich" for a man. Women also add "a" to the end of their father's last name. So Lidiya Ivanovna Radionova is the daughter of Ivan Radionov.

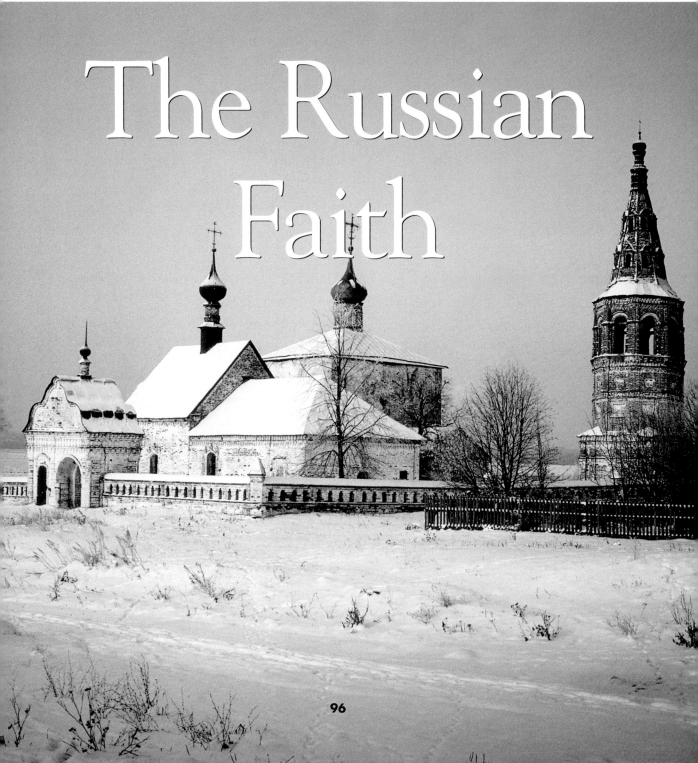

The Russian Faith

NDER THE CZARS, THE RUSSIAN GOVERNMENT USED THE church as a way to control the people. Under the Soviets, religion was condemned as "the opiate of the masses" and eventually almost outlawed. More than 75,000 churches were closed, made into warehouses, left to decay, destroyed, or put to other use. Some of the most famous churches, including St. Basil's Cathedral just outside the Kremlin in Moscow, were kept in good condition and converted to museums of atheism to promote anti-God beliefs.

Opposite: **A church in the Suzdal region of Russia**

A Precious Icon

Icons—paintings of Jesus Christ, the Virgin Mary, or saints—are displayed in Orthodox churches on altar screens called iconastases. Some of these icons are believed to have miraculous powers. One of the most famous is *The Mother of God of Vladimir*, painted by Saint Luke. This icon is thought to be one of three portraits of the Virgin Mary painted during her lifetime. It was taken to Constantinople from Jerusalem in the fifth century and then sent to a Russian prince in Kiev during the 1100s. The prince took it with him on a military campaign, but the horses carrying the icon could not cross the Kliasma River. Believing this was a sign from God, he built a church there to house the icon. Czars were crowned in front of it, and a later prince, Andre, carried it on a victorious military campaign. It was later credited with saving the city of Moscow from three different attacks. Pilgrims still bring offerings to place before the icon.

A congregation at an Easter night service

For all the years when the Communists held power, only the elderly dared to be seen in the few open churches. Worship meant risking one's job or even arrest. The beautiful buildings crumbled and priceless icons were stolen, sold by the government to foreign collectors for "hard" currency, or left to rot in damp abandoned buildings. Some priests went "underground" and held private worship services in secret, traveling from village to village.

After the fall of the Soviet state, the Orthodox faith made a strong and immediate comeback. Churches reopened, with congregations made up largely of older people who had remained faithful. Young men began entering the priesthood, and young families helped repair crumbling village churches. They baptized their children, and church weddings and funerals became popular.

Aleksei II (1928–)

Born Aleksei M. Ridiger, he was elected the Patriarch of the Russian Orthodox Church in 1990. This is the highest position in that faith, comparable to the Pope in Roman Catholicism. As head of the country's largest and most powerful religion, Aleksei has been a major figure in the rebirth of the Church in Russia, carefully forging a new relationship between the Church and the government. He has called the lack of spirituality "the greatest wound inflicted by the communist dictatorship."

Not everyone agrees on the reasons for this religious revival. Some believe it is a true outpouring of belief that lived despite the Soviets antichurch propaganda and persecution. Others wonder if it is not more of a cultural movement, with people seeking something truly Russian from their past to hang onto in a time of social change and economic confusion. Whatever the reasons, the rise of religion is dramatic: by 1993 there were more than 20,000 Orthodox churches in Russia compared to only 7,000 in 1988.

The Orthodox Church

The Russian Orthodox religion is observed with great ritual, much as is the Greek Orthodox faith. The two are part of a branch of Christianity known as the Byzantine or Eastern Rite, which has much in common with Roman Catholicism but observes many different rules and rituals. The Eastern Rite broke completely from the Church of Rome in 1054. This happened sixty-six years after Prince Vladimir forced all his subjects to be baptized into the church.

Although many Orthodox beliefs are close to those held by Roman Catholics, you would never mistake an Orthodox church service for a Catholic service. The first difference you would notice is that people stand instead of sitting or kneeling. Services last about two hours, sometimes several hours, but people stand the entire time. The church smells sweet with the smoke of incense, which is burned in round metal containers. These are swung on chains to spread the smoke through the air.

The Orthodox Year

Christmas	January 7
Baptism of Christ	January 19
Holy Friday	March or April
Orthodox Easter	March or April

Russian Easter Eggs

Easter is the major holiday in the Orthodox faith, even more important than Christmas. The Easter egg symbolizes the season, representing life beginning again—or the Resurrection of Christ. Families paint intricate designs on fresh eggs, often using a technique called pysanky. Delicate patterns are drawn on the shell in wax, and then the egg is dipped in dye. The color does not stick where the wax is, creating white lines. Then another design is added and the egg is dipped in a darker color dye. After several layers of color have been added, the wax is melted off over a candle and a beautiful multicolored design suddenly appears. People all over Russia give these to their family and friends.

In the days of the czars, a family of jewelers named Fabergé created beautiful jeweled Easter eggs with tiny scenes inside them. Wealthy nobles and the royal family exchanged these instead of the painted eggs given by the common people.

Instead of speaking, the priest chants, and the only music is the human voice. Priests and their helpers wear long robes, and the priests often disappear into an inner sanctuary, hidden from the people by a wall called the *iconostasis*. This wall is covered with icons, paintings representing Christ, the saints, the prophets, and festivals of the church. Only priests can go behind it, entering through the Royal or Holy Door in its center. In addition to this wall of icons, the rest of the church is heavily decorated with pictures that help teach the lessons of the faith. Services are very solemn and formal, and the people

Decorated walls and pillars inside the Kremlin Assumption Cathedral

Religious Affiliation in the Federation

(Of Those Who Practice a Religion)

Russian Orthodox	59%
Muslim	36%
Other Christian	3%
Jewish	.01%

do not take much part in the ceremonies. The rich pageantry of the Russian Orthodox service represents the deep emotional feelings the Russians have for their religion, which they associate with their love for their homeland and their sense of "Russianness."

Other Faiths

A small minority of Russians worship at other churches, mostly other sects of the Eastern Orthodox faith or Roman Catholic. The few Protestant Christians in Russia are mostly Lutherans or Baptists. With a history of persecution of Jews, it is not surprising that most Jews have emigrated elsewhere. There are only about a hundred synagogues in all of Russia. Many of Russia's Jewish people do not observe their faith by going to synagogue. Followers of Islam, though common in the eastern states, are comparatively few in western Russia, but they do have a mosque in Moscow.

Since churches have again been allowed to operate in Russia, many missionaries have arrived from Europe and the Americas. These represent many faiths from Roman Catholic to Jehovah's Witnesses. The revival of other religions worries the Russian Orthodox leaders. In 1993, the Patriarch, head of the Russian Orthodox Church, urged the Duma to pass a law limiting who could preach by requiring other religions to register with the government.

Most of the Russian Federation's Muslim population lives outside of Russia in the republics to the south. Muslims in these states are largely "secularized" and do not observe the strict codes required in purely Islamic states. Women do not have to wear veils, and businesses can stay open on Fridays. However, Islam, too, has undergone a revival that worries Russian leaders. Islamic fundamentalists are involved with the rebellion in Chechnya, and Russian leaders fear that increasing ties with Islamic countries will fuel anti-Russian opinion there and in the autonomous republics of Tatarstan and Bash Korostan.

The curious stop to listen to a sidewalk preacher.

Russia's Rich Culture

104

Music is a high priority for Russians, despite the many hardships they have had to endure just to survive. Even the Soviet government was generous in its support of Russia's famous ballet companies, its orchestras, and other performers. In 1995, it was estimated that Russia had 470,000 theaters.

Music got off to a slow start in Russia because of the rules of the Orthodox Church. Only the human voice could be heard in worship, and that was limited to the same chants. Music outside the church was, according to Orthodoxy, the work of the devil. The first musical traditions began in the mid-1600s when Peter I brought European musicians to his court. By the 1700s, the court had its own theater, orchestra, and opera house.

The first works of Russian composers showed the influence of their musical training in Italy, but after Napoleon was defeated in 1812, Russian national pride soared and composers began to create a truly Russian style. This was the era of the great Russian musicians Peter Tchaikovsky, Modest Mussorgsky, Alexander Borodin, and Nikolai Rimsky-Korsakov. Their works were clearly Russian, rich in the melodies and tones of ancient folk songs. However, music was still for the aristocracy; until 1859 public concerts could only be held for five weeks out of the year.

Music and Politics

The Communists ordered musicians to write only cheerful songs that people could sing and songs about the struggle of workers or revolutionary fighters. Upset by these restrictions, many talented composers left Russia. The best known from the early years of the Soviet regime are Igor Stravinsky, Sergei Prokofiev, Sergei Rachmaninoff, and Dmitri Shostakovich. Only the last of these remained in Russia.

Also during this time, the government helped to spread music to the common people, building theaters and concert halls throughout the land and making live performance of music and ballet a popular entertainment. Ballet and music schools produced outstanding performers, and students who showed promise were encouraged, educated, and given jobs.

Today, as in other areas of the arts, these formerly state-supported schools and musical groups are having a hard time finding money to continue. With the government no longer paying the salaries of artists, many talented people have turned to other ways to earn a living. The sounds of foreign pop music are often heard, but the sounds of Russian rock also fill the air.

Composer and conductor Igor Stravinsky

The Rock Scene

Moscow's young pack the basement rock and jazz clubs or bang heads to punk or acid rock. Despite the fact that Russians prefer to hear popular American or European stars, some Russian groups have made it to the top. The hard rock band Tequilajazz is from St. Petersburg, and Mumms Troll, a band from Vladivostok plays highly original rock.

Popular Russian pop star Vladimir Presnacov

Russian Ballet

Probably no place in the world is more famous for its ballet dancers as Russia. The Bolshoi in Moscow and the Kirov in St. Petersburg are the best known ballet companies in the world. The years of artistic suppression under the Soviets,

Students at ballet practice

Two Ballet Greats

Rudolf Nureyev (1938–1993) (left) and Mikhail Baryshnikov (1949–) (right) both trained at the famous Leningrad Kirov school of ballet and were Russia's leading male dancers. But the restrictions on life and art in the Soviet Union and the rigid classical styles of the Kirov Ballet prompted each in turn to leave Russia and pursue his career in the West. Baryshnikov brought ballet to the Hollywood screen as a star of the film *White Nights*.

however, prompted many of Russia's greatest dancers to defect to the West, including Rudolf Nureyev, Mikhail Baryshnikov, and the premier ballerina Natalia Makarova.

Russian dancers are celebrities, and their performances are packed with enthusiastic audiences. Perhaps the best known ballerina of the twentieth century was Anna Pavlova (1881–1931). During the Soviet period Galina Ulanova and Maya Plaisetskaya were stars of the Leningrad-Kirov Ballet. Altynai Asylmuratova, of the Kirov company, became Russia's most popular ballerina in the 1990s.

World-Class Writers

Russia's literary heritage has endured more setbacks than its other arts, since writers were often feared by governments who thought that they would spread "dangerous" ideas. As in art, the earliest writing was done in monasteries, where monks wrote of the lives of the saints. Under the czars, when contact with Europe was encouraged, such great writers as Alexander Pushkin, Fyodor Dostoyevsky, Leo Tolstoy, Anton Chekov, and Nicolai Gogol produced many works that put Russia on the literary map.

These nineteenth-century writers described the world they saw around them, the hypocrisy of the nobility, the poor living conditions of the peasants, and the inhumanity of serfdom. They also wrote of the Russians' deep love for their land and the magic that they find in the woods of the taiga. By describing Russian life as it really was and not as the czar saw it, the writers were regarded

Leo Tolstoy

as dangerous troublemakers. Nicolai Gogol's *Dead Souls*, about a man who buys the identity papers of dead serfs from landowners for a scheme to make money, showed how little the nobles cared about the serfs. After reading it, people had even less respect for the landowners.

Writing the Party Line

Although writers were often censored by the czars or even exiled for writing about political subjects, these limitations were nothing compared to what would happen to writers during the rule of the Communists. Under the Soviets, writers were encouraged to write what the state wanted. Called Socialist Realism, these works were all much alike and told stories of worker-heroes. Many writers refused to write such tales and carried on the traditions of those who came before them. Writers like Solzhenitzyn chose to write about the horrors of communist rule, telling of the prison slave camps. He was tried for treason after writing *Gulag Archipelego* and was sent to a labor camp. He was later exiled, moving to Switzerland and the United States; he returned to Russia only after the 1991 revolution.

Boris Pasternak was cut off from work after writing about the horrors of the 1917 revolution in *Doctor Zhivago*. He died in Moscow in 1960, never having seen the book published in his own country. It became a best-seller and a popular movie in the West.

Literature in the Soviet Union almost died until Khrushchev lifted some restrictions, but even then writers could not go too far. Boris Pasternak and Alexander

Solzhenitsyn are examples of what happened to those who crossed the line. Only since the 1991 revolution have writers dared to create original works, but the economy is so bad that it is hard to find publishers—or readers to buy them.

Tales of the People

Generations of parents and grandparents have preserved Russia's folktales by telling and retelling them to their own children and grandchildren. Many of the tales teach moral lessons of the triumph of good over evil, lessons that are often quite different from the events in the real lives of the people. Several tell of encounters with the witch Baba Yaga. One, retold in the book *Baba Yaga and the Wise Doll*, tells how a little girl outsmarts her two wicked sisters and the witch, with the help of a doll.

These folktales can be found in literature, music, and even art. The best-known musical version is found in Prokofiev's *Peter and the Wolf*, in which the composer introduces different musical instruments to represent each character.

Folk and Fine Arts

The best-known form of Russian painting is the icon (see Chapter Eight, The Russian Faith), and old examples of this art are highly prized by collectors and museums. Other early church decoration, usually painted directly on the walls, is being restored after years of neglect.

While only a few Russian painters and sculptors—Vasili Kandinsky and Marc Chagal among them—are well known

Matryoshka dolls on display

in the rest of the world, the bright round shapes and smiling faces of *Matryoshka* (pronounced mat-ROOSH-ka) dolls have become almost a symbol of Russia. Sets of matching dolls fit one inside the other, in sets that may have more than a dozen dolls. Artists buy these plain wooden egg-shaped boxes in sets, then paint them to look like

One of the World's Greatest Art Museums

Art lovers everywhere have heard of Russia's giant treasure house of world art, The Hermitage in St. Petersburg. The main building, with 1,057 rooms, was the czar's Winter Palace. It was decorated by the private art collection of Peter the Great, and the collection was continued by Catherine the Great. More art, taken from the homes of nobles and wealthy people after the 1917 revolution, was added to the collection. Only a small percentage of the museum's contents are shown to the public at any time, but it has such a vast collection that whole galleries are filled with the works of a single major artist. The museum is best known for its paintings by the French Impressionists and other European painters.

women in traditional dresses and scarves. Some are works of art, with each doll's face and dress painted in intricate detail. More recently, sets of these painted to look like Russian leaders have been made to sell to tourists.

Sports Fans

Through all their troubles, Russians have been enthusiastic about sports. Even small towns have sports facilities where children can learn soccer, basketball, volleyball, hockey, gymnastics, and track skills. Stadiums and playing fields are common sights, and soccer is by far the favorite game.

An instructor gives pointers at the Vokresinsk hockey school.

The Soviet state supported athletes preparing for the Olympics, providing them with sports training just as other students studied math or science. Competition was fierce among this sports elite for a place on the Olympic or other competitive teams. Russians brought home many gold and silver medals, often breaking Olympic records. More than 25,000 athletes and 1,200 coaches were paid by the government to prepare for these amateur events. Salaries of athletes were disguised as military or other government jobs so that they would not be considered professionals and ineligible for the Olympics.

The men's gymnastic team celebrate their gold medals at the 1996 Summer Olympics.

In the 1992 Albertville, France, and Barcelona, Spain, Olympics, Russian athletes and athletes from other Soviet states were left suddenly without a country to represent, so the Olympic Committee made a special designation for them called "Combined Team." They did well, and for the first time, the free world cheered for them wholeheartedly. The eighty-seven medal winners had no national flag to be raised at the awards ceremony and carried for the closing ceremony, so they carried the Olympic flag instead. Since then, Russian athletes have had to work for a living while training for their sport without government help, just like athletes from other countries. At the Summer Olympics in 1996 in Atlanta, Georgia, Russian athletes still placed third overall, winning sixty-three medals. Twenty-six of these were gold, six of them in men's swimming events.

Several top Russian hockey players have moved to the United States or Canada, where they play for National Hockey League teams. Slava Fetisov was a star of the Red Army team before joining the New Jersey Devils in 1989. He now coaches for that team. Pavel Bure, "The Russian Rocket," also left the Red Army team and plays for the Florida Panthers. Defecting directly after the Red Army's victory in the 1989 World Championships, Alexander Mogilny played for the Buffalo Sabres before joining the Vancouver Canucks.

Millions of Russians play chess regularly, a game they learn in school from the first grade because it is considered to be good mental exercise. Public parks are often filled with men playing chess, and Russian players frequently win the world championships.

Gary Kasparov (1963–)

Not many countries consider their chess champion a national sports hero, but when Gary Kasparov won the Soviet championship at age 18 and followed it by becoming world champion when he was only 22, his name was known all over Russia. He was outspoken in his support of government reform, while the man he defeated, Anatoly Karpov, supported the Communists, so Kasparov's victory became a political symbol as well.

Now that people are allowed to practice religion openly, the Orthodox faith has returned as a way to observe life's great events. Holidays, which became more political than cultural under the Soviets, now include the Christian celebrations of Christmas and Easter.

Baptism and Funeral Customs

Baptisms are becoming common as more and more Russians are returning to their faith. This is a joyful day when all the relatives and friends gather at the church. The baby wears a long white dress, and everyone stands around the baptismal font, a large decorated basin filled with holy water. After the service, the family invites everyone to a feast to celebrate the new baby.

A Russian Wedding Custom

It is not at all unusual to see brides in their white dresses laying a bouquet of flowers on the Tomb of the Unknown Soldier inside the Kremlin, at the memorial to those who died in the Siege of Leningrad, at St. Petersburg or another war memorial in a public park. It is a good omen for the future to pay respects to the past.

When a Russian dies, instead of having "calling hours" at a funeral home, the body is taken to the church and placed near the altar. The family stays close to pray and to greet friends who visit the church to console them and pray for the person who died. Candles are lighted in their memory. In a large church there may be several caskets lined up in front of the altar at the same time, with families and friends praying beside each of them.

Mourners attend a funeral service.

Life in Russia

For most Russians, except those in the still-privileged upper layer of society, the message "you must give up the good life today so that life will be better tomorrow" is just as much a part of life now as it was under the Soviets. Three generations of Russians have lived under this code and are still waiting for things to get better.

Although daily life is still very difficult, without doubt many things have changed for the better. Just being able to talk openly about problems and possible solutions is a new experience for most Russians. Like every other part of Russian life, even the daily rhythms of family, work, school, and play are in transition.

Russians at Home

One of the worst problems facing Russians today is the lack of housing, a problem that originated in the Soviet era. It is common for three or four couples and their children to share a very small apartment. Many families have grandparents, parents, and grown children (and often their young children as well) living together. Most have at least two families in an apartment.

More than 5 million people who cannot find or afford an apartment of their own live in communal apartment buildings, where dozens of people share four or five bathrooms and kitchens. Since 1992, the government has been privatizing government-owned housing, so many people now own their own apartments, small as they are.

Some people have tiny *dachas*, buildings in the country, where they go on weekends and where grandparents and young children stay in the summer. Here they tend gardens that provide the family with food. These unheated dachas are only habitable during the summer, but give families a short time with more privacy and space. Everyone looks forward to this "vacation" from overcrowded living.

Vacations are spent at family dachas.

Small villages near big cities are growing fast, as new construction companies hurry to build small homes. The demand for these homes is so great that it is impossible to build them fast enough. About three-fourths of Russians live in cities, so it will be a long time before housing there catches up with the demand.

Although people who live in the country can often raise much of their own food, their living conditions are no better. Their small wooden homes are often without water, indoor toilets, or electricity.

New homes are built to meet the growing demand for housing.

A babushka and her grandchildren

Family Life

One benefit of the crowded living conditions is that Russian families are very close. Children know their grandparents, who often take care of them while both parents work. Cousins are playmates, aunts and uncles are like second parents. Children are lovingly cared for and in a poor family are often better dressed than their parents. Most families have only one or two children—more would mean even more overcrowding in tiny apartments.

Grandmothers, called *babushkas*, are an important part of family life. They care for children, help with housework and shopping, and often contribute to the family budget by working part time. With both parents working to provide enough money to live on, children often know their grandmothers better than their own mothers.

Friends are important to Russians, who visit each other often and share what little they have freely. Guests are made welcome with a special meal, even when it is prepared with the last food in the house. A typical Russian greeting for guests is to present a loaf of bread and a dish of salt on a tray that has been covered with an embroidered cloth. Guests break off a piece of bread, dip it in the salt, and eat it.

Young People

While small children are well cared for by their many relatives, adolescents find little entertainment in Russian towns and cities. Sports are popular after-school and weekend activities, and most of the big cities have recreational facilities. Pick-up sports games are also popular with young people. Some, though, find life boring and have turned to street gangs, drinking, or drugs to fill their spare time. These problems, which began during the Soviet era, have become worse with the uncertainty of economic and social change. Poverty and the breakdown of government-provided health care has left some children ill, abandoned, and homeless.

Goods from the West

No longer does everyone have to line up to shop in state-owned stores to buy dreary dark-colored clothes and cheap merchandise. Today, the lines are in front of private shops offering stylish clothes and goods from Europe and America.

Lavish goods are available to some Russians.

A free-market economy has created another shopping option for Russians. Under the Soviets, it was illegal for a citizen to sell anything he had not made or grown himself. In 1992 this law was repealed, and it didn't take long for Russians to catch onto the idea of a "middleman" who could legally move needed goods from place to place.

Smart businesspeople now buy goods in the cities where they are manufactured and sell them on the streets of other cities where these goods are scarce. Distribution of goods was so poor under the Soviets that food often rotted before it could leave the place in which it was grown. With the breakdown of that system, people must create their own methods of distribution. Low-cost goods from China and other neighboring countries are also available now, usually smuggled in and sold in street markets. Although these items are cheap, they are known for their low quality.

From this trade, a new wealthy merchant class has grown. Just as under the Soviets, some people are doing very well, but the majority of Russians have only the bare essentials. Although Russians can shop for modern goods, for labor-saving home appliances, and for stylish, colorful clothing—once things only the communist elite could have—few can afford to buy them. Low pay for most jobs means that few Russian people have enough money to buy luxury goods or even expensive necessities.

What Russians Eat

The typical Russian diet is made up of bread and cereals, potatoes, cabbage, seasonal vegetables, and small amounts of meat.

Favorite Foods

While the food is solid and plain (spices are rarely used), there are several dishes typical of Russia and its neighboring countries that are favorites wherever they are found. *Bliny* are thin pancakes served with jam, meat, or sour cream. Beef Stroganoff is a delicious stew of beef in a rich, creamy sauce. *Pirozhki* are meat or vegetable dumplings that may be boiled like ravioli, baked, or fried. The Ukrainian soup called *borscht*, made of beets, cabbage, and meat, is also a popular dish in Russia. For breakfast (and also at other meals), Russians enjoy a hearty cooked buckwheat cereal called kasha.

This meat is usually of very poor quality and contains a lot of fat. Fresh fruits and vegetables are rare and expensive. The average Russian eats as much as 70 percent more calories daily than Americans do.

This woman prepares a large meal for her family.

Those with land can grow their own food. Others must pay the fast-rising prices for basics that were once provided cheaply by the government. Until Boris Yeltsin took the controls off prices, they had been frozen at the same level for almost thirty years. Prices began to rise, until families were paying six to ten times more for necessities like milk.

Time for Relaxing

While eating out is expensive, Russians, especially men, spend time in cafes, which are the social centers of city neighborhoods and larger towns. Here they drink, watch television (still rare in homes), and carry on long discussions, often about politics and philosophy.

Life in Russia **125**

Russian Holidays

New Year's Day	January 1
Christmas Day	January 7
Defenders of the Motherland Day	February 23
International Women's Day	March 8
Orthodox Easter	March or April
Victory Day	May 9
Independence Day	June 12
Anniversary of the new democratic state	August 21
October Revolution Day	November 7

Soccer, as already noted, is the most popular spectator sport, and fans line up regularly to see the Moscow Spartak, one of the most popular teams in the country. During the long winters, Russians enjoy skating, sledding, ice hockey, and cross-country skiing. Hockey is especially popular and many Russian players have become international stars. The long cold winters ensure that there is plenty of ice to practice on. Children bundled up into thick winter clothes are a common sight tumbling in the snow and building snowmen.

Children have fun in the snow.

Circus Time

Russians particularly like the circus. Acrobats balance on prancing horses, aerial artists walk high above the ring on ropes, fierce-looking lions jump through rings—all to the delight of audiences of all ages. Tickets are very cheap, and nearly every city has a circus or an arena for traveling troops. The Moscow Circus is the largest, with more than 7,000 performers.

Ussuri tigers perform at the circus.

Timeline

	2500 B.C. Egyptians build the Pyramids and the Sphinx in Giza.
	563 B.C. The Buddha is born in India.
	A.D. 313 The Roman emperor Constantine recognizes Christianity.
	610 The Prophet Muhammad begins preaching a new religion called Islam.
Slavs occupy eastern European Plain. **Pre-800**	
Byzantine Christianity approved as state religion by Vladimir. **988**	
	1054 The Eastern (Orthodox) and Western (Roman) Churches break apart.
	1066 William the Conqueror defeats the English in the Battle of Hastings.
	1095 Pope Urban II proclaims the First Crusade.
Prince of Suzdal captures Kiev, power shifts to the northeast. **Early 1200s**	1215 King John seals the Magna Carta.
Second Tartar invasion, beginning of Tartar rule and the Golden Horde. **1235**	
	1300s The Renaissance begins in Italy.
	1347 The Black Death sweeps through Europe.
End of the rule of the Golden Horde. **1480**	1453 Ottoman Turks capture Constantinople, conquering the Byzantine Empire.
	1492 Columbus arrives in North America.
Ivan IV (Ivan the Terrible) becomes Czar. **1533**	1500s The Reformation leads to the birth of Protestantism.
Michael Romanov named Czar. **1613**	
Serfdom established. **1649**	
Peter I, The Great, becomes Czar. **1682**	
Catherine II, The Great, crowned. **1762**	
	1776 The Declaration of Independence is signed.
	1789 The French Revolution begins.
Serfs freed. **1861**	1865 The American Civil War ends.

Russian History

Nicholas II crowned.	**1894**
Bloody Sunday, massacre of peasants.	**1905**
First Duma elected.	**1906**
World War I begins, and Russia enters.	**1914**
Czar abdicates, provisional government formed, Bolsheviks seize power.	**1917**
Lenin dies, Stalin becomes leader and starts his purges of party members.	**1924**
Stalin signs treaty with Hitler; Soviets invade Poland, Latvia, Lithuania, and Estonia, and part of Finland.	**1939**
Germany attacks Soviet Union; Soviet Union joins the western Allies against Germany.	**1941**
Stalin dies, Khrushchev era begins.	**1953**
Berlin Wall built: first manned orbital space flight by Yuri Gagarin.	**1961**
Soviet Union invades Afghanistan.	**1979**
Mikhail Gorbachev named general secretary.	**1985**
Policies of glasnost and perestroika announced.	**1986–1987**
Berlin Wall taken down, end of cold war.	**1989**
Russia declares its sovereignty, Yeltsin named president.	**1990**
CIS founded, Soviet Union ceases to exist.	**1991**
Vladimir Putin elected president.	**2000**

World History

1929	Worldwide economic depression begins.
1939	World War II begins, following the German invasion of Poland.
1945	World War II ends.
1957	The Vietnam War starts.
1969	Humans land on the moon.
1975	The Vietnam War ends.
1983	Drought and famine in Africa.
1992	Bill Clinton is elected U.S. president.
2000	George W. Bush is elected U.S. president.

Fast Facts

Official name: Russian Federation

Capital: Moscow

Official language: Russian, but local nationalities may use their languages.

Russia's flag

Siberia

Official religion:	None
Year of founding:	1991
National anthem:	Not yet agreed upon.
Type of government:	Federation with a strong president and two-chamber legislative body.
Chief of state:	President
Head of government:	Prime minister
Area:	6.63 million square miles (17 million sq km)
Latitude and longitude of geographic center:	Novosibirsk, at 55° north by 83° east
Bordering countries:	In Asia: Kazakhstan, Mongolia, China, North Korea. In Europe: Finland, Estonia, Latvia, Belarus, Ukraine, Georgia, and Azerbaijan
Highest elevation:	Mount Elbrus, 18,510 feet (5,642 m), in the North Caucasus Mountains.
Lowest elevation:	Sea level
Average temperatures:	Oymyakon, in Siberia -96°F (-71°C) December. Astrakhan, on the Caspian Sea 88°F (31°C) July.
Average annual rainfall:	0.44 inches (1.12 cm) Verkhoyansk (Yakutiya) Sakha Republic; 4.5 inches (11.43 cm) Sochi, Krasnodar Territory
National population (2000 estimate):	150 million

Hermitage Museum

Population of major cities:

St. Petersburg	5,130,000
Volgograd	2,702,000
Novosibirsk	1,478,000
Yekaterinburg	1,300,000
Smolensk	1,166,000

Famous landmarks:

- ▶ *The Kremlin*, Moscow
- ▶ *St. Basil's Cathedral*, Moscow
- ▶ *Hermitage Museum*, St. Petersburg
- ▶ *Peter and Paul Fortress*, St. Petersburg
- ▶ *Admiralty*, St. Petersburg
- ▶ *Millennium Monument*, Novgorod
- ▶ *Chapel of St. Nicholas*, Novosibirsk
- ▶ *Alexander Nevsky Cathedral*, Novosibirsk

Industry: The top Russian exports are oil and natural gas. Production of steel and iron is declining but is still high. Products include machinery for industry and agriculture and consumer products, including foods, clothing, automobiles, and computers. Russia also produces large quantities of minerals and timber.

Currency: The ruble is made up of 100 kopecks. There are approximately 31.20 rubles to US$1.

System of weights and measures: Metric

Literacy rate: 99 percent

Currency

Class discussion

Andrei Sakharov

Common words and phrases:

Zdravstvuite (ZDRAST-voo-yet-eh)	Hello	
Pozhalvista (pa-ZAHL-oos-ta)	Please	
Da Svidanie (das-vee-DAHN-ya)	Goodbye	
Da (dah)	Yes	
Nyet (nee-et)	No	
Spasibo (Spah-SEE-bo)	Thank you	
Menia zovut ... (min-Ya-AH-za-VOOT ...)	My name is ...	

Famous Russian people:

Sergey Diaghilev *Ballet choreographer*	(1872–1929)
Nikolai Gogol *Novelist and short story writer*	(1809–1852)
Vladimir Lenin *Revolutionary, Soviet ruler*	(1870–1924)
Boris Pasternak *Novelist, literary translator*	(1890–1960)
Peter the Great *Czar, Peter I*	(1672–1725)
Andrei Sakharov *Physicist, social activist*	(1921–1989)
Leon Trotsky *Revolutionary, philosopher*	(1879–1940)

To Find Out More

Books

- Andreev, Tania. *Food in Russia*. International Food Library. Vero Beach, FL: Rourke Publications, Inc, 1989.

- Federal Research Division, Library of Congress. *Area Handbook Series, Russia— A Country Study*. Washington, DC: Library of Congress, 1996.

- Kendall, Russ. *Russian Girl*. New York: Scholastic, Inc., 1994.

- Kent, Deborah. *Moscow*. Danbury, CT: Children's Press, 2000.

- Kirchner, Walther. HarperCollins *College Outline: Russian History*. New York: HarperCollins Publishers, 1991.

- Kort, Michael. *Nations in Transition*. Russia. New York: Facts on File, 1995.

- Kort , Michael. *The Handbook of the Former Soviet Union*. Brookfield, CT: Millbrook Press, Inc., 1997.

- Oram, Hiawyn (retold by). *Baba Yaga and the Wise Doll*. New York: Dutton Children's Books, 1999.

- *Russia, Then and Now*. Minneapolis: Lerner Publications Co., 1992.

Videotapes

- *The Face of Russia* (Public Broadcasting System, 1998). Video Finders, 425 East Colorado Blvd, Glendale CA 91205, 800-343-4727

- *My Name Is Ivan* (Mosfilm Studios Production, Fox-Lorber Home Video, 1963). Tells the story of an orphan who spies behind enemy lines during World War II. In German and Russian with English subtitles.

Web Sites

▶ **General Information**
www.oldrussia.net
*Illustrated stories from old Russia
including* Baba Yaga *and* Vasilla
the Beautiful.

▶ **Russian National Tourist Office
Guide to Russia**
www.russia-travel.com
*Information on history, embassies,
museums, photos, and tours such as
the Trans-Siberian Express.*

▶ **CIA, the World Factbook**
www.cia.gov/cia/publications/
factbook/geos/rs.html
*Good general information about Russia
with history, government organization,
and economic statistics.*

▶ **Bank of Russia**
www.cbr.ru/eng/bank-notes_coins/
bank-notes/today/history/central-
bank.asp
*Good information on the economy
and the currency, includes a full
description of the money wtih pictures.*

▶ **Moscow Guide**
www.moscow-guide.ru
*A good source that tells about the
city, history, currency, information.
Check under culture for virtual tours.*

▶ **Library of Congress Country
Studies**
http://lcweb2.loc.gov/frd/cs/cshome.
html
*The Web site of the Library of Congress
with the Web version of the Country
Studies book.*

▶ **U.S.. Department of Agriculture**
www.ers.usda.gov/briefing/russia/
data_ag_ataglance.htm
Agricultural information.

▶ **University of Toronto**
www.friends-partners.org/
oldfriends/mes/russia.html
*News and general information
on Russia.*

Embassies

▶ **Embassy of the Russian Federation**
2650 Wisconsin Avenue, NW
Washington, DC 20007
(202) 298-5700

▶ **Embassy of the Russian Federation**
285 Charlotte Street
Ottawa, Ontario K1N 8L5
Canada
(613) 235-4341

Index

Page numbers in *italics* indicate illustrations.

Meet the Author

STILLMAN D. ROGERS has traveled extensively throughout Europe, Central and South America, and North America. He has written several travel guidebooks, most recently the *Adventure Guide to Canada's Atlantic Provinces*, *Adventure Guide to the Chesapeake Bay*, and *Signpost Guide: Portugal*. He has written and illustrated children's books describing the lives of young people in Zambia, Peru, and South Africa. Stillman is co-author of Enchantment of the World books *Canada* and *Zimbabwe*, wrote Cities of the World *Montreal*, and co-authored *Toronto* and *Vancouver* for that series.

He is a graduate of Harvard College and earned his doctorate degree at American University.

He has been interested in Russia, its history and culture, since studying about it in college. Russian novels are among his favorite reading. His travels in Russia have taken him on canal and river systems throughout the countryside and have given him an appreciation for the land and its long-suffering people. "The history of the people of Russia is a long tale of betrayal by their leaders," he says, "and I have great hope that the people of Russia may finally be breaking free from their long enslavement."

Photo Credits